"Bible-study habits go
the retelling of a rema
the gospel in the page
readable account of 1
amazing grace will both encourage and instruct you."
   —**Joel Belz**, Founder, *WORLD* magazine

"This is a book that lingers. Not only did I frequently stop reading and spend time reflecting and praying, but I continue to ponder and celebrate the deep wonders of the gospel in the beautiful story of Naaman's slave girl. This riveting read is now on my list of favorite books."
   —**Susan Hunt**, Speaker, Author, and Former Director, Women's Ministries in the Church (PCA)

"What I particularly like about Mark's book is that it reminds us that God's ways are not our ways, nor is his method of reconciliation the same as the world's. Naaman's slave girl acts much like Christ. She brings reconciliation through humility and servanthood, rather than through special strategies of communication. She shows that in God's economy, weakness is really strength, and that by deferring to others, one can intervene and bring about a redemptive reconciliation."
   —**Paul D. Kooistra**, President, Erskine College and Seminary

"Using this beautiful Old Testament presentation of the gospel, Mark Belz woos us to be reconciled to God and man. While Mark is a masterful Bible teacher, his real effectiveness in charting the journey to wholeness comes from his having walked it with Jesus."
   —**George Robertson**, Pastor, First Presbyterian Church, Augusta, Georgia

"For some reading this book, the narrative found in 2 Kings 5 will be familiar. For others, it is about to become familiar. This historical event not only anticipated the New Testament clarity of the gospel of saving grace in Christ, but also demonstrated and announced the gospel message and ministry of reconciliation. Mark Belz unfolds this story with energy and theological clarity."

—**Harry L. Reeder III**, Senior Pastor, Briarwood Presbyterian Church, Birmingham, Alabama

A JOURNEY TO
WHOLENESS

THE GOSPEL ACCORDING TO
THE OLD TESTAMENT

*A series of studies on the lives
of Old Testament characters, written for
laypeople and pastors, and designed to
encourage Christ-centered reading, teaching,
and preaching of the Old Testament*

IAIN M. DUGUID
Series Editor

After God's Own Heart, by Mark J. Boda
Crying Out for Vindication, by David R. Jackson
Faith in the Face of Apostasy, by Raymond B. Dillard
From Bondage to Liberty, by Anthony T. Selvaggio
From Famine to Fullness, by Dean R. Ulrich
Hope in the Midst of a Hostile World, by George M. Schwab
Immanuel in Our Place, by Tremper Longman III
Inconspicuous Providence, by Bryan R. Gregory
A Journey to Wholeness, by Mark Belz
Living in the Gap between Promise and Reality, by Iain M. Duguid
Living in the Grip of Relentless Grace, by Iain M. Duguid
Living in the Light of Inextinguishable Hope, by Iain M. Duguid
    and Matthew P. Harmon
Longing for God in an Age of Discouragement, by Bryan Gregory
Love Divine and Unfailing, by Michael P. V. Barrett
Recovering Eden, by Zack Eswine
Right in Their Own Eyes, by George M. Schwab
Salvation through Judgment and Mercy, by Bryan D. Estelle

A JOURNEY TO WHOLENESS

THE GOSPEL ACCORDING TO
NAAMAN'S SLAVE GIRL

MARK BELZ

P U B L I S H I N G
P.O. BOX 817 • PHILLIPSBURG • NEW JERSEY 08865-0817

Unless otherwise indicated, all Scripture quotations are from the Holy Bible, New International Version®. NIV®. Copyright © 1973, 1978, 1984, 2011 by Biblica, Inc®.Used by permission. All rights reserved.

Scripture quotations marked (ᴇsv) are from the ESV® Bible (*The Holy Bible, English Standard Version®*), copyright © 2001 by Crossway. 2011 Text Edition. Used by permission. All rights reserved.

Italics within Scripture quotations indicate emphasis added.

ISBN: 978-1-62995-063-1 (pbk)
ISBN: 978-1-62995-064-8 (ePub)
ISBN: 978-1-62995-065-5 (Mobi)

Printed in the United States of America

Library of Congress Cataloging-in-Publication Data

Belz, Mark.
 A journey to wholeness : the gospel according to Naaman's slave girl / Mark Belz. -- 1st ed.
    pages cm. -- (The Gospel according to the Old Testament)
 Includes bibliographical references and index.
 ISBN 978-1-62995-063-1 (pbk.)
 1. Bible. Kings, 2nd, V--Criticism, interpretation, etc. 2. Naaman, the Syrian. 3. Reconciliation--Biblical teaching. 4. Reconciliation--Religious aspects--Christianity. I. Title.
 BS1335.52.B45 2015
 222'.5406--dc23
                                          2014046285

For
Barry and Ann Henning
slaves to the gospel of reconciliation

CONTENTS

SERIES FOREWORD

*The New Testament is in the Old concealed;
the Old Testament is in the New revealed.*
—*Augustine*

Concerning this salvation, the prophets who prophesied about the grace that was to be yours searched and inquired carefully, inquiring what person or time the Spirit of Christ in them was indicating when he predicted the sufferings of Christ and the subsequent glories. It was revealed to them that they were serving not themselves but you, in the things that have now been announced to you through those who preached the good news to you by the Holy Spirit sent from heaven, things into which angels long to look. (1 Peter 1:10–12)

"Moreover, some women of our company amazed us. They were at the tomb early in the morning, and when they did not find his body, they came back saying that they had even seen a vision of angels, who said that he was alive. Some of those who were with us went to the tomb and found it just as the women had said, but him they did not see." And he said to them, "O foolish ones, and slow of heart to believe all that the prophets have spoken! Was it not necessary that the Christ should suffer these things and enter into his glory?" And beginning with Moses and all the Prophets, he interpreted to them in all the Scriptures the things concerning himself. (Luke 24:22–27)

The prophets searched. Angels longed to see. And the disciples didn't understand. But Moses, the Prophets, and all the Old Testament Scriptures had spoken about it—that Jesus would come, suffer, and then be glorified. God began to tell a story in the Old Testament, the ending of which the audience eagerly anticipated. But the Old Testament audience was left hanging. The plot was laid out, but the climax was delayed. The unfinished story begged for an ending. In Christ, God has provided the climax to the Old Testament story. Jesus did not arrive unannounced; his coming was declared *in advance* in the Old Testament—not just in explicit prophecies of the Messiah, but also by means of the stories of all the events, characters, and circumstances in the Old Testament. God was telling a larger, overarching, unified story. From the account of creation in Genesis to the final stories of the return from exile, God progressively unfolded his plan of salvation. And the Old Testament account of that plan always pointed in some way to Christ.

AIMS OF THIS SERIES

The Gospel According to the Old Testament series was begun by my former professors, Tremper Longman and Al Groves, to whom I owe an enormous personal debt of gratitude. I learned from them a great deal about how to recognize the gospel in the Old Testament. I share their deep conviction that the Bible, both Old and New Testaments, is a unified revelation of God and that its thematic unity is found in Christ. This series of studies will continue to pursue their initial aims:

- to lay out the pervasiveness of the revelation of Christ in the Old Testament

- to promote a Christ-centered reading of the Old Testament
- to encourage Christ-centered preaching and teaching from the Old Testament

These volumes are written primarily for pastors and lay-people, not scholars. They are designed in the first instance to serve the church, not the academy.

My hope and prayer remain the same as Tremper and Al's: that this series will continue to encourage the revival of interest in the Old Testament as a book that constantly points forward to Jesus Christ, to his sufferings and the glories that would follow.

IAIN M. DUGUID

FOREWORD

I first learned of Mark Belz's interest in the narrative of the healing of the Syrian general Naaman when in June 1992 I heard him deliver his moderatorial address to the General Assembly of my church, the Presbyterian Church in America. Proof of the impression made on me by that address is a note that I entered in the margin of my Bible at 2 Kings 5: "Gehazi's action changed the news that Naaman took home. When Naaman, back in Aram, told his story, he would no longer say that the gift had been free—the flesh may glory a little in his presence." A keen insight!

What you will find in this book is a time-honored form of biblical exposition in which a particular narrative is expounded in depth, the history brought to life with the addition of background, context, and collateral detail, and its various lessons drawn out. This is the kind of work that used to be very popular with thoughtful Christians. Alexander Moody Stuart's *The Three Marys* is a specimen of this art; so is George Lawson's *The History of Joseph*. On a larger scale, we might think of F. W. Krummacher's *Elijah the Tishbite* or James Stalker's *The Life of St. Paul*. Those are older works, harder for twenty-first-century Americans to read, but they were works much beloved of the deeper sort of Christian for the way they drew from biblical narratives lessons for the life of faith.

It is high time that such works should be furnished for a new generation of readers, for if we have learned anything about the Word of God over the past generation, it is how artfully its histories were written and how intentionally the biblical writers communicated theology, ethics, and wisdom in, under, around, and through their narratives. More subtle and implicit than, say, Paul in his letter to the Romans, the author of *Kings* was nevertheless every bit as much a theologian as the great apostle to the Gentiles and as much a preacher of the gospel of Jesus Christ. I have found through years of preaching the biblical narratives that God's people find the lessons of these histories as easy to grasp as in the straightforward exposition of the prophets and apostles and often feel the force of their truth more powerfully because in the narratives the truth is personalized, depicted in flesh and blood. We may not find a John 3:16 in the Old Testament, but where, pray tell, is that good news more beautifully expressed and commended to faith than in 2 Kings 5? Here is the conversion of Zacchaeus and of the apostle Paul, but with so much interesting psychological detail. A man in need, a message to be believed, a believer transmitting the message, the gift of grace, the promise of healing, the necessity and the challenge of faith, the power of God, the confession of Yahweh as Lord, a changed life, even a baptism—it is all here in 2 Kings 5.

Mark Belz is a man who knows of what he speaks and has done a beautiful job of drawing out from one of the most beautiful narratives in the Bible the most beautiful truth in the world.

ROBERT S. RAYBURN, PH.D.
Pastor, Faith Presbyterian Church (PCA)
Tacoma, Washington

PREFACE

Some parts of Scripture do not yield well to an outline, and I believe the passage presented here is one of them. For some reason, 2 Kings 5 has interested me for more than two decades, and because it is narrative, a story, and because it didn't happen in an outline, it has increasingly seemed best to me to exegete it "as it sits," and not impose something on the passage that is not there.

Of course, the truths gleaned from the story can be organized, and a different level of understanding is gained by doing so. That, however, is the task of systematic theology, and the story of Naaman's healing is not systematic. So perhaps one of the reasons I've chosen not to organize or outline the passage is that I am anything but a systematic theologian.

Writing a book is much like building a house. There are two ways to do it: with plans and without. I've never been adept at planning anything, so after lengthy consideration of all the pros and cons, and bouncing the issue off many of my friends, I opted for no plans. We'll see how that approach works out.

Whether three or ninety-three, everyone loves a story. I've noticed that when a preacher begins to tell a story from the pulpit, drowsy eyes open, heads swivel, and people look straight at him. No matter whether they had heard a word he said before, they want to see how the story turns out. Some might not even much care how the sermon turns out! We are quickly drawn in when a story is told. Surely this is one of the reasons that Jesus himself resorted so often to parables.

We also remember stories. Outlines have to be memorized, but stories do not. The reason for this is that human beings, by nature, are more interested in events than theories. Our lives *are* stories, not outlines; real experiences, not math. We are people, and stories are about people. If you read 2 Kings 5 even once, you will be able to close the Bible and tell the story to your children. Try this with the first chapter of your high school algebra book, and you'll get the idea!

Stories also illustrate—they make things clear. In this story, the healing of Naaman, we will find that old gospel truths, the subject of systematics, are colored in and clarified for us. For example, when we say that "salvation is by grace alone," we state a wonderful, bedrock truth. But we are helped immensely when we see that illustrated when a poor prophet, standing on his front lawn, refuses to take bars of gold and silver from a repentant sinner. *That* is what "salvation by grace alone" means in real life, and we understand it best by illustration.

My hope is that the reader might benefit not so much from any insight that the author may have, but from what the story itself teaches. It is just one chapter, and in a way may seem isolated from the rest of Scripture. While it does stand on its own feet, I think you will find it exciting to explore the ways in which it relates to and exemplifies so many truths found elsewhere in Scripture, as well as so many issues confronting us in the world today. In other words, I hope you find it as exciting as I have.

ACKNOWLEDGMENTS

I am not just being polite in acknowledging those who have aided me in composing this book. Being an inexperienced writer, I greatly needed every one of them and profited immensely from the help that each gave.

Maybe it's not typical, but in 1964 I fell in love with my bride, Linda, in significant part because she could write like no one else. She has fervency and is able to articulate ideas powerfully. Unfortunately, she hasn't written nearly enough in her life, but she has helped others to do so, particularly her husband. Thank you to the love of my life.

My son Aaron is a poet and writer. His father thinks he is good at it, as do many others. Aaron has attempted to bring me up to date as far as style is concerned and has aided in many other ways. He has urged me to push ahead when I flagged, and encouraged me every step of the way. Aaron, I needed that.

The most kindly but ruthless help came from my good friend and law-school classmate John Stonebraker. He accepted my request that he, an accomplished author, read the manuscript and make whatever suggestions he desired. He read the whole thing (poor man) in detail and, for the most part, did not make suggestions but issued orders. By way of example, one of them, which I initially resisted, was to eliminate most of the semicolons that I had inserted in the first manuscript. John e-mailed me and said that I "was singlehandedly attempting to revive the archaic use of the semicolon." Not wanting to appear archaic, I removed most of them. You could say that he performed a "semicolonectomy" on the author, and without anesthesia.

But in this and myriad other ways, he greatly improved the writing and did so without remuneration. Thank you, John.

Finally, I must thank my six-year-old granddaughter, Hannah, who would often prod me along by asking, "Grandpa, when are you going to finish making your book?" This question sent me right back to my Bible and laptop. Now that it's written, Hannah and I have time to sit on the couch and read someone else's book.

CHAPTER ONE

THE STORY

OVERVIEW

This is a story, recorded in 2 Kings chapter 5, of the prophet Elisha healing a Syrian general of leprosy. It is a story, and I will refer to it as such as we progress through it. But like many stories, it is also history, a true story. It's not a parable, although it has many similarities to the parables that Jesus preached. The characters are real people. The nations involved were real nations at a particular time in world history, more than eight hundred years before the birth of Jesus. It's reliable as a historical record because it was written by good historians and by the inspiration of the Holy Spirit.

We know that the Lord has preserved this event in the written Word because, like all Scripture, it is profitable for us—"for teaching, rebuking, correcting and training in righteousness" (2 Tim. 3:16). It illustrates, in real lives, the truth, principles, and dynamics of the gospel. It shows God's sovereign interest and power in salvation and in making the gospel available to everyone, long before New Testament times. The story is about God's overarching grace in the gospel, bridging the chasms between slave and owner, Jew and Gentile, prophet and pagan, God and man.

1

THEME AND FOCUS

The theme of this writing is the ministry of reconciliation, which the apostle Paul claimed as his own in 2 Corinthians 5, and the focus is the Syrian general's little Jewish slave girl. She is sometimes forgotten as this story is recounted, perhaps because she is mentioned only once. But in fact, she is the protagonist. Without this unnamed child's testimony to her mistress, there would have been no healing and no story.

The story comprises the whole of 2 Kings 5. As one reads that chapter, the author's compact style is immediately evident. There is a wonderful economy of language that begs to be "unpacked." And we know it was meant to be unpacked because Jesus himself unpacked some of it in Luke 4. That is, its meaning, its application, and its prophetic nature go far beyond the story itself. For the person even passably acquainted with the rest of Scripture, one reading of Naaman's story will conjure up all kinds of thoughts regarding what he or she already knows about the gospel. The story resonates.

JORDAN RIVER

The Jordan River is central to the event because it is where Naaman's healing occurred. The river is important throughout Scripture, and to this day is associated with cleansing, healing, and crossing over. John the Baptist preached in the wilderness, commanding his hearers to repent of their sins, and he baptized those who listened and obeyed in the Jordan River. Jesus himself was baptized by John the Baptist in the Jordan. For us, water baptism signifies, among other things, cleansing from sin, and the Jordan has always carried this meaning. Ricky Skaggs, a contemporary Kentucky bluegrass singer, characterized the Jordan's cleansing power like this: "I'm going down to the River of Jordan/And let the cool waters cleanse my soul," and noting that Naaman saw that "the cool waters made him whole."[1]

The river also conveys a "crossing over"—its meaning from the fifteenth century B.C. forward, when the Israelites crossed as a nation into Canaan. This landmark in Jewish history became a symbol for all believers, representing not only death—crossing over from this earthly life to heaven—but the new birth as well, experienced in this life and at death. This is the "crossing over" that Jesus talked about when he said:

> Very truly I tell you, whoever hears my word and believes him who sent me has eternal life and will not be judged but has crossed over from death to life. Very truly I tell you, a time is coming and has now come when the dead will hear the voice of the Son of God and those who hear will live. (John 5:24–25)

The river sometimes represents healing, although it was a surprise to me, as I studied this story, that Naaman's is the only scriptural record of physical healing in the Jordan River. In fact, Naaman's healing there is one reason that thousands of people have made pilgrimages to the river even to this day, hoping they, too, will receive healing. To Christians, the river has become a symbol of spiritual healing and transformation, and as we "cross over," we are cleansed and made fit for entrance into the kingdom:

> When I tread the verge of Jordan,
> Bid my anxious fears subside;
> Death of death and hell's Destruction,
> Land me safe on Canaan's side.[2]

All three of these symbolic aspects of the Jordan River—cleansing, crossing over, and healing—are relevant to the story of Naaman the Syrian. In this episode of God's supernatural action, Naaman was cleansed of his sin, crossed over from death to life (John 5:24), and was healed. He received every blessing of God's salvation in Christ.

TEXT

This story is just a sliver of Jewish history. It records an unusual occurrence in Israel—the northern kingdom—about two hundred years after Solomon's magnificent kingdom had collapsed and been divided. It's a story about disease and healing, riches and poverty, unbelief and faith, smallness and greatness, weakness and strength, allies and enemies, slavery and freedom, lies and truth, worship and sacrilege, the common and the holy—even church discipline. Though written compactly, it is a wonderful and riveting story. Whether you have read it or not, please read 2 Kings 5 through again (or for the first time) before you read this book; I've included the entire chapter below. And if time doesn't permit you to read this book, skip it!—and just ponder the story itself.

Imagine this as a play. The story begins with a mighty Syrian military officer, an enemy of Israel, afflicted with leprosy, a dread disease. The proud but diseased enemy officer enters from stage left. During the story, this mighty Syrian is healed. At the end of the play, when the final curtain descends, the military officer exits stage right, now humbled, healed physically, and—astonishingly—a member of the family of God. He had been an enemy of that family but was now fully reconciled to them and to their God.

The story is a powerful example of the gospel of reconciliation. As the story develops, we will see the gospel light shining brighter and brighter until we can see an Old Testament example of what the prophet Isaiah was referring to when he said:

The people walking in darkness
   have seen a great light;
on those living in the land of deep darkness
   a light has dawned. (Isa. 9:2)

We will see this truth in action here: God's saving grace is extended to a Gentile. It's a foreshadowing of the great opening of the gospel to the Gentiles recorded in the book of Acts. It becomes evident that when the apostle Paul said that "God was reconciling the world to himself in Christ, not counting people's sins against them" (2 Cor. 5:19), he was not referring exclusively to the era following the death and resurrection of Christ. It is God's eternal purpose to reconcile the world—both Jew and Gentile—to himself and to one another, and here we find that he was doing so eight hundred years before Jesus came to earth.

For ready reference as we begin the discussion of this story, here is the text:

2 KINGS 5

¹ Now Naaman was commander of the army of the king of Aram. He was a great man in the sight of his master and highly regarded, because through him the LORD had given victory to Aram. He was a valiant soldier, but he had leprosy.

² Now bands of raiders from Aram had gone out and had taken captive a young girl from Israel, and she served Naaman's wife. ³ She said to her mistress, "If only my master would see the prophet who is in Samaria! He would cure him of his leprosy."

⁴ Naaman went to his master and told him what the girl from Israel had said. ⁵ "By all means, go," the king of Aram replied. "I will send a letter to the king of Israel." So Naaman left, taking with him ten talents of silver, six thousand shekels of gold and

ten sets of clothing. ⁶ The letter that he took to the king of Israel read: "With this letter I am sending my servant Naaman to you so that you may cure him of his leprosy."

⁷ As soon as the king of Israel read the letter, he tore his robes and said, "Am I God? Can I kill and bring back to life? Why does this fellow send someone to me to be cured of his leprosy? See how he is trying to pick a quarrel with me!"

⁸ When Elisha the man of God heard that the king of Israel had torn his robes, he sent him this message: "Why have you torn your robes? Have the man come to me and he will know that there is a prophet in Israel." ⁹ So Naaman went with his horses and chariots and stopped at the door of Elisha's house. ¹⁰ Elisha sent a messenger to say to him, "Go, wash yourself seven times in the Jordan, and your flesh will be restored and you will be cleansed."

¹¹ But Naaman went away angry and said, "I thought that he would surely come out to me and stand and call on the name of the LORD his God, wave his hand over the spot and cure me of my leprosy. ¹² Are not Abana and Pharpar, the rivers of Damascus, better than all the waters of Israel? Couldn't I wash in them and be cleansed?" So he turned and went off in a rage.

¹³ Naaman's servants went to him and said, "My father, if the prophet had told you to do some great thing, would you not have done it? How much more, then, when he tells you, 'Wash and be cleansed'!" ¹⁴ So he went down and dipped himself in the Jordan seven times, as the man of God had told him, and his flesh was restored and became clean like that of a young boy.

¹⁵ Then Naaman and all his attendants went back to the man of God. He stood before him and said, "Now I know that there is no God in all the world

except in Israel. So please accept a gift from your servant."

[16] The prophet answered, "As surely as the LORD lives, whom I serve, I will not accept a thing." And even though Naaman urged him, he refused.

[17] "If you will not," said Naaman, "please let me, your servant, be given as much earth as a pair of mules can carry, for your servant will never again make burnt offerings and sacrifices to any other god but the LORD. [18] But may the LORD forgive your servant for this one thing: When my master enters the temple of Rimmon to bow down and he is leaning on my arm and I have to bow there also—when I bow down in the temple of Rimmon, may the LORD forgive your servant for this."

[19] "Go in peace," Elisha said.

After Naaman had traveled some distance, [20] Gehazi, the servant of Elisha the man of God, said to himself, "My master was too easy on Naaman, this Aramean, by not accepting from him what he brought. As surely as the LORD lives, I will run after him and get something from him."

[21] So Gehazi hurried after Naaman. When Naaman saw him running toward him, he got down from the chariot to meet him. "Is everything all right?" he asked.

[22] "Everything is all right," Gehazi answered. "My master sent me to say, 'Two young men from the company of the prophets have just come to me from the hill country of Ephraim. Please give them a talent of silver and two sets of clothing.'"

[23] "By all means, take two talents," said Naaman. He urged Gehazi to accept them, and then tied up the two talents of silver in two bags, with two sets of clothing. He gave them to two of his servants, and they carried them ahead of Gehazi. [24] When Gehazi came to the hill, he took the things from the servants

and put them away in the house. He sent the men away and they left.

²⁵ When he went in and stood before his master, Elisha asked him, "Where have you been, Gehazi?"

"Your servant didn't go anywhere," Gehazi answered.

²⁶ But Elisha said to him, "Was not my spirit with you when the man got down from his chariot to meet you? Is this the time to take money or to accept clothes—or olive groves and vineyards, or flocks and herds, or male and female slaves? ²⁷ Naaman's leprosy will cling to you and to your descendants forever." Then Gehazi went from Elisha's presence and his skin was leprous—it had become as white as snow.

THEME OF RECONCILIATION

As we progress through the story, we will gain just an inkling of the eternal bond formed when we are reconciled with God in Jesus Christ and reconciled with one another. That "double bonding" appears in seed form in the story of Naaman, a prototype of the truth made explicit in years to come, but even in seed form, it is profound. The two bonds are inseparably intertwined; reconciliation with God will always mean reconciliation with one another, and true reconciliation with one another cannot exist apart from reconciliation with God. It has been said that the ground at the foot of the cross is perfectly level, and that is so. The apostle Paul summarized it thus:

> So in Christ Jesus you are all children of God through faith, for all of you who were baptized into Christ have clothed yourselves with Christ. There is neither Jew nor Gentile, neither slave nor free, nor is there male and female, for you are all one in Christ Jesus.

8

If you belong to Christ, then you are Abraham's seed,
and heirs according to the promise. (Gal. 3:26–29)

FOR FURTHER REFLECTION

1. What are some reasons that this story was included in the Bible? Upon first reading, can you identify other parts of Scripture that it relates to?
2. How would you characterize the theme, or themes, of this story? How does it fit in with the overall message of the gospel? Does it echo any other themes found in the Bible?
3. As the story is told, is there anything in it that comes as a surprise to you?
4. Before reading 2 Kings 5, what popped into your mind when you heard the words *Jordan River*? Do you think your ideas are related to what happened in this story?
5. In a very general way, what do you think this story has to say about God's relationship to different races, and about different races' relationships to one another?

CHAPTER TWO

THE GENERAL

THE MAN NAAMAN

Naaman was a military man at the zenith of his career. He was a Syrian commander over the troops of Aram, of which Damascus was the capital. He served Ben-Hadad, the king of Aram. Because of his victories on the battlefield, Naaman had earned the high confidence of the king, who regarded Naaman as a "great man" (2 Kings 5:1). The king held him in high esteem because of his strong character, which was fit for the task of being a "valiant soldier." Worldly success was Naaman's, "but he had leprosy" (v. 1).

Naaman's background is not recorded; we don't know whether he was of humble or noble birth or what his training and experiences were. But as a military commander, he was unusually accomplished, evidenced by the victories he achieved for Ben-Hadad. We do not have a record of Naaman's exact military campaigns, or of particular victories that he achieved. But we are told that he had made his nation, Aram, victorious. We also know from other Scripture that some of these victories came at the expense of Israel's northern kingdom, and that the Lord God was helping Naaman gain prowess as a military man.

It may seem strange that the Lord was giving victory to Aram, Israel's principal enemy at the time. They were a heathen people who did not know the God of Israel. But God works in mysterious ways. The Lord had done this at other times in Israel's history, too. When Israel first entered the Promised Land, God did not let his chosen people immediately drive out all the Canaanites, but said:

> "Because this nation has violated the covenant I ordained for their ancestors and has not listened to me, I will no longer drive out before them any of the nations Joshua left when he died. I will use them to test Israel and see whether they will keep the way of the Lord and walk in it as their ancestors did." The Lord had allowed those nations to remain; he did not drive them out at once by giving them into the hands of Joshua. (Judg. 2:20–23)

Later, it was the Lord himself who appointed Babylon to sack Jerusalem, and the Jews' resistance to Babylon's invasions was counted as disobedience; those who resisted would die (Jer. 21:9). One of the saddest statements in Scripture, probably the lowest spot, at least to that date in Israel's history, is this: "It was because of the Lord's anger that all this happened to Jerusalem and Judah, and in the end he thrust them from his presence" (2 Kings 24:20). But the Lord was not through with his people, and there is comfort in these words as well, because in this severe discipline there is evidence of his care:

> My son, do not despise the Lord's discipline,
>   and do not resent his rebuke,
> because the Lord disciplines those he loves,
>   as a father the son he delights in. (Prov. 3:11–12)

Jeremiah's warning to the Jews in Jerusalem not to resist Babylon was, in substance, the same: "do not despise the Lord's discipline, and do not resent his rebuke." You will see, now or later, that it is meant for your good, Jeremiah told them. " 'For I know the plans I have for you,' declares the Lord, 'plans to prosper you and not to harm you, plans to give you hope and a future' " (Jer. 29:11). In these examples, neither the Canaanites nor the Babylonians were aware that the Lord was causing them to succeed against Israel. They trusted in their own gods and were not aware of the true commander in chief. Nor is there any evidence that Naaman realized that it was the Lord who was directing his brilliant military career.

NAAMAN'S RELATIONSHIP TO GOD

Naaman, like every other human being, had a relationship with the Lord. He did not know about the relationship, but he had one nevertheless. Naaman led his troops against Israel and was Israel's enemy. He worshiped not the Lord, but Aram's false god, Rimmon. Naaman did not know the Lord, even though the Lord knew him and gave him success. In one battle against Israel and Judah, recorded in 1 Kings, Ahab the king of Israel was killed when an Aramean arrow, shot "at random," pierced his armor. In that case, the Aramean's success in taking Ahab's life had nothing to do with human military skill or strategy. Even the Syrian soldiers thought it was a lucky break, but it wasn't. God arranged events to give the Syrians victory. It is likely that Naaman at least heard of this victory; he might have fought in the battle, although his participation isn't mentioned in the Bible. Whether or not Naaman took part in the battle, the Lord was arranging events in his life, but Naaman had no idea just how active the Lord would be.

Naaman thought he understood something about the God of Israel, but what he knew was pretty much wrong. He did not think of Jehovah as anything more than a local god—one of many. In 1 Kings 20, we are told that the military establishment in Aram developed a particular view of Israel's God after Aram and Israel faced each other in a battle in the mountains. Israel prevailed, leaving the defeated army of Aram searching for answers.

After some consideration, the Syrian military decided that this confrontation revealed that the gods of Israel must have been the gods of the mountains (obviously, because Israel had won the battle): "Their gods are gods of the hills, and so they were stronger than we" (1 Kings 20:23 ESV). So the Arameans altered their strategy and determined that next time they would fight Israel in the plains, where Aram's gods would have a better shot at victory.

This was conventional wisdom at the time. Gods were many, and they were parochial. A person just had to figure out their particular zip code and assign the work to a god who had expertise in the situation at hand. To anyone who would pay attention and use his head, the gods could be manipulated or sidestepped. These gods might be valuable for a good strategist who knew how to use them, but they were limited, local. Anyone wily enough could manipulate the situation to avoid them or to employ them for protection and victory. Naaman, as chief officer of Aram's military, doubtless assumed this view, and it was his job to work his way around the God of Israel. But in doing this, he revealed the fact that he did not know or understand Israel's God.

Naaman believed that the gods, including Israel's God, were like chess pieces. He didn't have a clue that the God of Israel was sovereignly and intimately involved in his life. The God of Israel was at work not only in the mountains but in the plains, in Aram—everywhere. It was the Lord himself who was giving Naaman successes and failures. It was the Lord who caused his sovereign to hold him in high esteem. (As we will later see, this "high esteem" will prove to be important in the story.) The God of Israel was the One arranging the events, just as he did earlier as recorded in the book of Exodus. God instructed Moses to tell Pharaoh: "But I have raised you up for this very purpose, that I might show you my power and that my name might be proclaimed in all the earth" (Ex. 9:16).

TROUBLE AND SALVATION

A person is often unaware of the Lord's present work in his life, coming to see it only later in the rearview mirror. Some years ago, I was talking to an elder in a church in Michigan. It was late afternoon, and we were sitting in his backyard fronting a lake. The legendary North Woods mosquitoes had just come in for their evening bombing run. I asked this elder how long he had been a Christian and how he came to faith in Christ. He sat back in his lawn chair for a bit, slapping away the mosquitoes, and then began his answer: "Well, the first time I noticed the Lord at work in my life was 1958."

As a believer looks back, he can see it. The realization comes upon us, we put the pieces together, and then we are amazed at how God had arranged events and used other people to bring us into the kingdom. An anonymous poet has written:

> I sought the Lord, and afterward I knew
> He moved my soul to seek him, seeking me;
> It was not I that found, O Savior true;
> No, I was found of Thee.[1]

For some years I attended a men's Wednesday lunch at a local church in St. Louis. Each week one of the men was called on to give his testimony. The testimonies had a common thread: there had been some trouble, some event that was hard to comprehend, some injury or sickness, a financial catastrophe, or even a disaster that had preceded conversion. One man's little girl had drowned in a swimming pool. One had received life-threatening injuries in an automobile accident. One had cancer. Another was forced to take bankruptcy. Another was in bed for months and, for the first time in his life, read through the Bible—twice. In each of these cases, the trouble in life had brought about the realization that he had lost control and encountered something he could not solve on his own.

A member of our church told me how he came to faith in Christ. He and his wife lived in Dallas at the time. Not knowing the Lord, they were frustrated in their marriage and in pretty much everything else in their lives. At a friend's constant urging, and in order to get the pesky friend off their backs, he and his wife began attending a church where they heard the gospel. The sermons did not altogether convince him, but he was getting on the right track. Then something happened that did convince him. One day, after he had attended a business meeting on the top floor of a thirty-something-story building, he got on the elevator to descend to street level. The descent turned out to be a bit faster than he anticipated. The elevator went into what felt like free-fall, finally shuddering to a stop at ground level. He says that all he knows is that when he left the top floor, he was not a believer, but by the time he reached the lobby, he was!

Coming in late one night from Cincinnati to the airport in St. Louis, our plane encountered a violent thunder and lightning storm. I was perfectly relaxed, of course, except for the fact that I was trembling all over while tightly clenching my teeth and watching my knuckles turn white. The two men sitting behind me were apparently in the same state of paralyzing fear because I heard one of them say to the other: "Time to say our Hail Marys!" Whether these two men experienced a subsequent change in their relationship with God, I don't know. But I can tell you that my friend's elevator scare was permanent and eternal, not just momentary. God often works eternal change in a person's brain and heart in this way. He can do it any way he wants.

For each of these people, it was the *trouble* that brought them to faith in Christ. Each one now has a personal understanding as to why John Newton, the former slave-trader, testified: "'Twas grace that taught my heart to fear, / And grace my fears relieved."[2] God does this, and often in his sovereign design permits Satan to instigate the trouble, for reasons that God has tailor-made for us, though we are suffering. It is not that he enjoys seeing us squirm or suffer. He is not sadistic. But he does keep us on the mat until we cry "uncle!" to ensure that in the end, after we wear ourselves out trying to solve the issue or get out of the trouble on our own, we understand that he was the One who met our need, who answered our cries when we were in deep distress. He gives us something very precious: gracious comfort in trouble. His rod and staff, in the end, always bring comfort (Ps. 23:4). They teach us that we are utterly dependent on him.

The pastor of a church that my wife and I attended in the late seventies said it this way:

> There is a young couple in our community. Both of them have graduate degrees. They do not know the Lord, but he has a good job and she is a stay-at-home mom, enjoying doing volunteer work in the school library. They have two beautiful, healthy children who are doing well in school; their house is paid for; he is getting regular promotions and their career objectives are all being met. They have a good reputation in their neighborhood. Everything in their lives seems to be going perfectly. Then something goes terribly wrong for them—*or worse, it doesn't.* (Tom Egbert)

There is nothing more tragic than an apparently happy but godless life that goes on without God's interruption.

NAAMAN'S TROUBLE

Naaman did not initiate his own salvation. He did not volunteer to contract leprosy. It was his slave girl who put forth the idea that he should see the prophet in Samaria. He was responding to things that came into his life apart from his own volition. But because of these things, he was forced to turn somewhere, to someone, for help. At this point in the narrative, Naaman is learning the first half of John Newton's line but knows nothing about the second. His fears are growing—not yet relieved. Later, he would discover that it was by God's grace that he had leprosy, that it was God's grace that taught his heart to fear.

Leprosy must have been devastating for Naaman. His disease was more than a passing medical problem. It was a serious, lifelong, degrading social disability. In his day, lepers were eventually quarantined, ostracized from society and often from their families. Naaman's disease meant that there would come a time when he would be cut off from everyone except other lepers. There were few ancient stigmas equal to a leper's stigma. Scripture provides a picture of what it meant for the leper under the Mosaic law:

> Anyone with such a defiling disease must wear torn clothes, let their hair be unkempt, cover the lower part of their face and cry out, "Unclean! Unclean!" As long as they have the disease they remain unclean. They must live alone; they must live outside the camp. (Lev. 13:45–46)

Outside the camp is no place for a general. His military career was most likely in jeopardy. His position as commander of troops involved close contact with his men. A leper could not put troops at risk. Naaman had been a successful general, and as the commander responsible for directing Aram's military, he was skilled at keeping his men and the strategic situation under control. He was accustomed to being the one who issued the orders and watched other people carry them out. But now he was in trouble, big time, and he knew it. He was face to face with something horrific in his life over which he had no control at all. The Bible simply reports: "but he had leprosy." He couldn't reverse his failing health. No matter how great his abilities on the battlefield, or how successful he was in every other aspect of his life, he was now forced to recognize his own powerlessness. His life was being turned upside down, and there was nothing he could do about it. Where could he turn for help?

OUR TROUBLES

Have you ever been there—when something devastating has come into your life, and there is not a single thing you can do about it? You can't do anything about it on your own, and worse, you discover that no one else can do anything about it either. Another person may be able to help you to a degree, and encourage you and pray for you. But you know that no human has the power to solve your problem. It's just there, and it's awful. One of the things you feared the most is happening to you, and you find yourself in a dark tunnel with no answers. And when you peer down that dark tunnel and see what you believe is a glimmer of light, suddenly even that light is snuffed out, and the darkness is darker than ever, so dark that you can feel it. You've hit bottom. Job was there:

> For sighing has become my daily food;
>   my groans pour out like water.
> What I feared has come upon me;
>   what I dreaded has happened to me.
> I have no peace, no quietness;
>   I have no rest, but only turmoil. (Job 3:24–26)

Leprosy is not sin, nor can we say that it is caused by sin. Yet it is a picture of sin. In Scripture, it often represents an uncleanness and an incurable condition. It results in isolation and loneliness. It clings to you and won't let go.

It eats away at you, is destructive, and goes deeper and deeper into your body. Ultimately, it leads to death. The prophet Isaiah wrote of this condition:

> Your whole head is injured,
>   your whole heart afflicted,
> From the sole of your foot to the top of your head
>   there is no soundness—
>   only wounds and welts and open sores,
> not cleansed or bandaged or soothed with oil.
>   (Isa. 1:5b–6)

The prophet is describing how hopeless our condition is when we are deathly ill and try to remedy our sickness our way. We are all sin-sick and have no cure apart from God's healing. That's bad enough, but like the Israelites in Isaiah 1, in the natural man we are dozing on the couch, assuming that things are just fine, not even conscious of our condition. But like Naaman, we are the walking dead. If God loves us, he will jar us awake. God loved Naaman, and by the time the narrative begins in 2 Kings 5, Syria's top general is wide, wide awake.

This condition for which Naaman had no solution would prove to be the pivotal point of his life. In a spectacular way, this would lead to his welcome into the kingdom of heaven. He would find that hitting bottom was, in God's economy, not such a bad place to be. Naaman was about to get the help he so desperately needed, and it would come from an unlikely source.

FOR FURTHER REFLECTION

1. Are you, or have you ever been, like Naaman insofar as things were going well for you? Have you ever felt that life was going so smoothly that it would continue unabated? As you look back on that time, do you

believe things were going as smoothly as you thought they were? Was that really a good time for you?

2. Have you ever been like Naaman in that something hard came into your life? What was it? Was it ultimately good for you? In what ways?

3. When you came up against something hard, more than a bump in the road, can you remember how you handled it? Did you turn to others? Did they fully resolve the predicament?

4. As you look back, were there specific ways in which God helped you? Be honest. If you can't say that God helped you, speak up!

CHAPTER THREE

SLAVE GIRL

A KIDNAPPED CHILD

The Syrians made regular raids against Israel, in part so that they could steal livestock, money, clothing, and human beings. In one of the raids, Naaman's guerrillas captured a little Jewish girl and forced her to go with them to Aram. Apparently her sole value to them was as a slave, because they made her one. This tender soul was now far from her home, helpless, oppressed, maybe even abused. What, she must have asked herself, is to become of me? Is there any chance that I'll see my mom and dad again? Are they still together? Are my brothers, sisters, and friends still there? Are they alive, or have they been killed?

It's hard to imagine a crime more unfeeling and inexcusable than what these raiders inflicted on this little girl. By brute force they ripped her from her home, from her security, from those she loved and who loved her, away from those she depended on and trusted, and then pressed her into slave service far from home. There were no telephone privileges. Naaman's men had kidnapped this child. They didn't give a snap about her. She was just a piece of property as far as they were concerned.

Yet all the amazing events disclosed in 2 Kings 5 unfold because of words coming from this child's mouth.

It's important to note that the context of this chapter, 2 Kings 5, is slavery—not just slavery in general, or slavery of a nation or ethnic group, but the slavery of one particular young lady. The injustice she was experiencing was very personal.

If we were writing a children's bedtime story about this girl, we would very likely construct it so that a brave little girl held as a slave—because of her strength of character and goodness and some pixie dust sprinkled in—would be freed of her servitude and reunited with her mother and father. Or perhaps she would be rescued from Aram's military after a kiss from a valiant prince from Israel, and then she would live happily ever after. I've never read a story to my children or grandchildren that ended in any other way. Children's books without happy endings just don't sell. But we didn't write the story, and that's not the way it was.

Crimes against children are considered to be particularly heinous, not only in the Geneva Convention and similar rules of war, but in the teachings of Jesus. He loved the little children, and warned that it would be better for a man to be dropped in the sea with a millstone tied around his neck than to offend one of these little ones (Matt. 18:5–6). Children are utterly dependent and trusting. They are easily led. To violate their trust, to abuse a child is, in Jesus' words, worthy of the death penalty. *Offend* may seem an inadequate description for what Naaman's men did here. They took advantage of a little girl who was utterly unable to resist or defend herself.

NAAMAN'S GUILT

Naaman was ultimately the guilty party. He was in command of the men who had kidnapped that little girl. Obviously, he knew they had captured her because she was serving as a slave in his household. He had the power to return her to her home country and to her family. Not only was he ultimately responsible for her capture, but he actively perpetrated the evil day by day, continuing to hold her captive for his own personal benefit.

Slavery is tyranny, and slave-owners are tyrants. In 1858, in the seventh Lincoln-Douglas debate in Alton, Illinois, Abraham Lincoln defined slavery, in whatever form it might appear, as tyrannical. The opposing political party, he said, contains

> all who positively assert that slavery is right, and all who, like Judge Douglas, treat it as indifferent and do not say it is either right or wrong. That is the real issue. That is the issue that will continue in this country when these poor tongues of Judge Douglas and myself shall be silent. It is the eternal struggle between these two principles—right and wrong—throughout the world. They are the two principles that have stood face to face from the beginning of time, and will ever continue to struggle. The one is the common right of humanity, and the other the "divine right of kings." It is the same principle in whatever shape it develops itself. It is the same spirit that says, "You work and toil and earn bread, and I'll eat it." No matter in what shape it comes, whether from the mouth of a king who seeks to bestride the people of his own nation and live by the fruit of their labor, or from one race of men as an apology for enslaving another race, *it is the same tyrannical principle.*[1]

Lincoln was talking about the tyranny of the heart. At its root, it is not a political or social phenomenon. In whatever form it may be manifest, it is still an individual, personal disorder, the seeds of which are in every one of us.

This is a truth that can help us in understanding Naaman's status at this time in his life. When in college

25

I took *two* semesters of logic, thus becoming very logical. We were taught to think propositionally, and the thinking would go something like this:

> *a*—Naaman was a tyrant
> *b*—tyrants are sinners
> *c*—sinners are slaves to sin
> *therefore*—Naaman was a slave

This is what Jesus was alluding to when he addressed the Jews, who claimed that because they were children of Abraham, they were free and "no man's slave." But Jesus replied, "Very truly I tell you, everyone who sins is a slave to sin" (John 8:34). So Naaman, the oppressor, was himself infinitely more oppressed than the little girl. He, too, was a slave and badly needed to be set free.

Syria's commander in chief now had two major problems. He was worried about the first, but likely not the second. He knew that he had leprosy, this life-threatening disease, and that was his great concern. He probably never recognized that he had a second problem, which was "blood on his hands," brought about by his abuse of authority and his continuing oppression of a young girl. He was in a medical predicament of which he was fully aware; worse, he was in deadly trouble because of his sin, although at this point he didn't appreciate that fact and probably had concerns only about the former.

Naaman was the chief terrorist who had raided this girl's family. He was the oppressor; she was the oppressed. He was strong; she was weak; he was the abuser and she the abused. His king held him in high regard, but King Ben-Hadad most likely didn't even know about her. Naaman commanded troops, but she had no authority. He issued orders; she took orders. He was the master; she was his slave—he owned her. He was at the top; she was at the bottom. We do not even know her name.

THE SLAVE GIRL'S CONCERN FOR NAAMAN

But Naaman is the one who was terminal. Astonishingly, this young slave girl was concerned for him. It is too mild to say that she should have been resentful and bitter. From a human standpoint, that is what we could expect. She could have wished the worst for him. He had taken her from her mom and dad. The leprosy, particularly if it would end in death, was exactly what he deserved. That would be justice.

But she did not have a typical human attitude. Aware of her master's leprosy, she exclaimed to Naaman's wife: "Would that my master would see the prophet in Israel! He would heal him of his leprosy!" Compressed into this short exclamation is a wealth of information about this unnamed slave girl.

Art Linkletter, an entertainer from a bygone era (being almost bygone myself, I remember him), had a show called *Kids Say the Darndest Things*. It's true, but that is not what we see here. This wish that her master would see the prophet in Israel is not one of those darndest things—not a cute, surprising utterance from a kid. Nor can it be explained merely because she was a good-natured child, though that she probably was.

Rather, this exclamation shows a sincere and deep-felt concern for her master, Naaman. She desired the best for him, and she did not want him to continue to suffer from this illness. Her concern was not dutiful or forced but came from her heart. Rather than wishing him harm, or his just due for capturing her, she expressed nothing but concern (she wanted him to be healed and urged him to go to Samaria to see the prophet) and hope (she was confident that if he went, the prophet would heal him).

It is as though she had attended Jesus' Sermon on the Mount. "You have heard that it was said, 'Love your neighbor and hate your enemy.' But I tell you, love your enemies and pray for those who persecute you, that you may be children of your Father in heaven" (Matt. 5:43–45). Or you might conclude that she had time-traveled forward a few centuries and read Paul's admonition in Romans 12:14: "Bless those who persecute you; bless and do not curse." She was a child, most likely with simple duties, living a drab, harsh life as a slave; but she had an understanding of her true nature and saw a much bigger, more exciting existence than what was visible in her circumstances. She could have sung these words with countless believers through the ages living lives like hers:

> Joy to find in ev'ry station,
> Something still to do or bear;
> Think what Spirit dwells within thee,
> What Father's smile is thine.[2]

It is obvious that this girl had a pure and sweet character, but it was more than that. Something, or Someone, was at work within her. So much about her can be drawn from her exclamation: "Would that my master would see the prophet in Samaria! He would heal him of his leprosy!"

FRUIT OF THE SPIRIT

Naaman's little slave girl showed *love*. Love is not just a feeling: it is real empathy and concern for another person. It is not particularly demonstrated in friendliness toward those who are friendly with you. Her love for Naaman, her "master," was utterly selfless. "If you love those who love you, what reward will you get? Are not even the tax collectors doing that?" (Matt. 5:46). She loved her enemy! She loved her oppressor, her kidnapper! And her exclamation is really a prayer for him. "Would that my master would see the prophet who is in Samaria!"—a petition heard in heaven that he would agree to go down to Israel and get healed.

This girl's wish for her master's healing demonstrates more than that she was an exemplary human being. In fact, the natural man would typically not say such a thing, not under these circumstances. It would be foolishness to help your enemy. Remember that Jesus said, "You have heard that it has been said, love your friends and hate your enemies." This was and is conventional human wisdom. But true wisdom, true love, is to "love your enemies; be good to those who despitefully use you." Where did this servant girl find this kind of love?

She was *joyful*. Her utterance was enthusiastic, encouraging, buoyant, and optimistic. How could a child have been joyful in these circumstances? This is not just a bubbly, effervescent personality at work. Her joy was real and deep. And what she was joyful about was her recollection of this exceptional man of God, the prophet in Samaria. She exuberantly, unabashedly, confidently, and happily urged her master to go see him and be healed. What was the source of her joy?

She demonstrated *peace*, in the most profound sense of the word, because she spoke peace. "And he shall speak peace unto the heathen" (Zech. 9:10 KJV)—precisely what she was doing, for Naaman was pagan. This is the essence of the declaration of the gospel to the Gentiles. "How beautiful on the mountains are the feet of those who bring good news, who proclaim peace, who bring good tidings, who proclaim salvation" (Isa. 52:7). She was in a foreign land far from her home, a meek and lowly maiden of Naaman's enemy, Israel, and she spoke peace to him. He comprehended little as to the dimension of this peace, but he was soon to experience it. When he later parted ways with Elisha, the great prophet told him to "go in peace" (2 Kings 5:19). This is the peace that passes understanding (Phil. 4:7). Where did this slave girl get this kind of peace?

She was *good*—not only a good little girl, but intentionally good toward another person, to Naaman. She understood his trouble and earnestly desired the best for him. This goodness was not just a function of personality. Nor was it a product of hard work. We may try on our own all we want, but our efforts will never bring about this kind of goodness. "Make a tree good and its fruit will be good, or make a tree bad and its fruit will be bad, for a tree is recognized by its fruit. . . . A good man brings good things out of the good stored up in him, and an evil man brings evil things out of the evil stored up in him" (Matt. 12:33–35).

In fact, natural man doesn't even want this kind of goodness. Why in the world would you ever wish that something very, very good would happen to someone who had treated you very, very badly—a person who had terrorized, kidnapped, and enslaved you? With nothing but continued slavery expected in return? I'm certainly not that way naturally—none of us are. To the natural man, this brand of goodness is naive at best, and more likely just stupid. Where in the world does this kind of goodness come from?

The answer is that these amazing qualities didn't come from "in the world."

I recently attended a Bible study class where one of the participants commented with certainty that the Holy Spirit had not appeared until the New Testament times. Many Christians have this idea, believing that the Pentecost described in Acts 2 initiated the Holy Spirit's presence in believers.

Without question, that day of Pentecost was a special outpouring of the Holy Spirit's power that initiated a new era of the church, but the Spirit was present and working on this planet long before that day. You don't have to go far in Genesis to see him: "and the Spirit of God was hovering over the waters" (Gen. 1:2). "Do not cast me from your presence or take your Holy Spirit from me," David prayed in Psalm 51. We see the Holy Spirit at work all through the Old Testament, and this story of Naaman gives us one clear instance of his work. We know he was at work here because this little slave girl shows the fruit of the Holy Spirit, and her love, joy, peace, and goodness are best described not as qualities that she possessed, but as fruit that she bore.

Listed in Galatians 5:22–23a, this fruit is "love, joy, peace, forbearance, goodness, faithfulness, gentleness and self-control." In this brief exclamation, she demonstrated this kind of fruit. The fruit did not come out of thin air or good DNA. It came from someone living in her. The fruit is proof positive that she had the Holy Spirit within her. It's an apple tree if it has apples on it.

HER FAITHFULNESS

The little girl was also *faithful*, in two ways. Mainly, she was faithful to the God of Israel. She was not embarrassed or timid in delivering her testimony about what God's prophet could do. She didn't say that "he might heal you," or "he could heal you," but that "he *would* heal you!" She considered the healing a done deal if Naaman would simply go to Israel and see the great prophet.

Knowing that she was filled with the Spirit explains why this servant girl said what she did. "A good man brings good things out of the good stored up in his heart, and the evil man brings evil things out of the evil stored up in his heart. For the mouth speaks what the heart is full of" (Luke 6:45; see also Matt. 12:33–35).

She was a child, and she had the faith of a child. It was simple, sure, and unqualified. This is the kind of faith that pleases the Lord: "Truly I tell you, anyone who will not receive the kingdom of God like a little child will never enter it" (Mark 10:15). We adults are often cluttered with worldly concerns about how a testimony of something supernatural might sound to an unbeliever. But we see none of this worry in the slave girl's exclamation. If she had been hedging her bets, she might have said, "You may have a hard time believing this, but I think there is someone in Israel who might be able to help you. I think it's worth a try." But she didn't give herself a way out. Nor did she use a studied, intellectual approach. In fact, she used no particular approach at all, except to state a fact of faith in God. She was absolutely faithful to God, without mincing words.

My dad, an Iowa farmland preacher, was this way. When I was about twelve, I went with him to the local auto shop to get our car fixed (it always needed fixing). Dad made it his practice to give a testimony wherever he went, and he had previously talked to the owner of the establishment several times about the gospel. The man was polite, but he was not a believer. On this occasion, Dad said to him, "Henry, have you gotten things straightened out with the Lord yet?" Dad tended toward bluntness. I can't remember Henry's response, but I do remember (sorry to say) that I looked down at my shoes—embarrassed—when Dad asked the question. I was afraid of what Henry might think of us. Even at twelve, I was planning to run for governor. Although I had not yet announced my candidacy, I already sensed that this was not the way to get votes. But my dad was not politically astute.

You can tell from reading her statement that Naaman's slave girl was not looking down at her shoes. She was looking her mistress straight in the eye.

She was faithful to God, and she was faithful to her master. She could justifiably have kept this secret, this good news about a special man who could heal her owner of his leprosy. But she displayed fidelity. This truth about the prophet in Samaria was good news, and she rightly assumed that it was good news for him as well as her. Obviously, as far as Naaman was concerned, this kind of personal loyalty and devotion to his well-being was entirely undeserved. Amazingly, this slave girl gets in his corner. She is with Naaman in his predicament and joins him in his battle against leprosy. She is in solidarity with Naaman. Solidarity is harmony or union of concern, sympathy, and fellowship of interests. In this way, she is in solidarity with God and with man, just as Jesus is.

She is, in fact, a mediator, because a mediator serves the real interests of opposing parties.

HER VIEW OF HER OWNER

What, or whom, did she see when she saw Naaman? He was her owner, of course. She also saw him as Israel's enemy. But in her childlike vision she saw someone well beyond those things. Those things were incidental, not who Naaman was. In terms familiar to students of philosophy, to her these worldly characteristics were *accidental*, not the *essence* of the man.

Those things that defined Naaman in a worldly way were not important to her right now. When she looked at her owner, she was looking at the image of God. Naaman was exactly like her—a human being, a member of the human race. Her focus was humble and plain, no clutter. She did not see him as black, white, Democrat, Republican, rich, poor, educated, unschooled, Jew, or Gentile. She saw a person who had leprosy, pure and simple. He needed help. She was his slave, but that didn't matter either.

There is nothing good about slavery. It is not one isolated offense against another, but an ongoing evil, a persistent, degrading oppression. But even within the context of slavery, the Lord prescribes conduct. "Serve wholeheartedly, as if you were serving the Lord, not people, because you know that the Lord will reward each one for whatever good they do, whether they are slave or free" (Eph. 6:7–8). Clearly, this little girl was living her life as a slave as if she were serving the Lord.

SHE TARGETED HIS LEPROSY

Her compassion was specific to his need. Saying that you love someone is great, but it is proved to be true when

33

it is made particular, and to a particular person. Naaman had leprosy, and this was his besetting problem in life. She spoke into that exact need. This is a foreshadowing of Jesus' entire healing ministry, including the time he healed a blind man on the road to Jericho. The man called out to Jesus, as he was passing by, and Jesus stopped and ordered that the man be brought to him. When he came near, Jesus asked him, "What do you want me to do for you?" "Lord, I want to see," he replied. Jesus said to him, "Receive your sight; your faith has healed you" (Luke 18:40–42).

We testify to the world through "word and deed." But too often we chop this in two, thinking that word is separate from deed. Jesus did not artificially separate the two. He heard a man crying out to him and asked the man to tell him what he wanted. The man didn't give a long-drawn-out, theologically correct answer, thinking that this might be what the rabbi was looking for. No theological exam. Rather, the blind man gave the simple, most obvious answer—an answer that every man and woman on the planet can understand: "Lord, I want to *see.*"

And this answer was exactly what Jesus was wanting to hear. Jesus did not say, "Of course you want to see, but what you really need is to come to faith in me. We'll talk about this visually impaired thing afterwards." Jesus knew that this poor man's immediate and obvious need was to be able to see, and the Lord was concerned to meet the man and help him at that level. When he gave him sight, it was far more than an object lesson: *Jesus healed his eyes because he was blind.* So it was with Naaman's slave girl. She didn't go into the greater subjects that might have been discussed. What she knew, and what her master knew, was that he had leprosy and needed to be healed. Like Jesus, she spoke directly into his need.

Look at what the apostle to the Gentiles said: "If your enemy is hungry, feed him; if he is thirsty, give him something to drink; for by so doing you will heap burning coals on his head" (Rom. 12:20). Or if your enemy has leprosy, cure his leprosy—or at least do what you can to meet that specific need, like urging him to see the prophet in Israel. Not "if he is thirsty, put your arm around him and tell him that you'll be praying for him" and then go on to meet your family for Sunday dinner.

It is not as though a drink of water, food, or healing from blindness or leprosy is the crux of the issue. Without debate, the blind man's most crucial need was to come to faith in Christ. His healing is not the end of the story, nor is healing the end of Naaman's story. But giving a person in need a direct remedy specific to that need—not just a general expression of sympathy or a theological lecture—shows personal concern and displays deep and true love for that person. It is an act that the hurting soul can understand and appreciate.

RISK AND FEAR

You put yourself at substantial risk when you express love for another person by offering help for a specific need that the person may have. It is much easier to say, "You'll be in our thoughts and prayers" than to say, "Can we help pay your electric bill this month?" When you mention the specific need and invite a response to that particular need, you may be asked for specific help, and that puts a burden on you, albeit a joyful burden. Jesus invited a specific response and got it. His invitation elicited a plea for specific help: "Lord, *I want to see.*"

This girl told her mistress that Naaman would be healed of his leprosy if he would make an appointment with the prophet in Israel. She was putting herself at risk in giving this assurance. What if they laughed her out of the room? What if she turned out to be wrong? But true compassion for another always involves real invest-ment, and investment means risk. Children don't much mind making such an investment because they don't fully appreciate the consequences. We can learn from them because our hang-up is that we fear the consequences. King David said:

> Through the praise of children and infants
>> you have established a stronghold against your
>> enemies,
> to silence the foe and the avenger. (Ps. 8:2)

Through the little girl's praise to the Lord, implicit in her enthusiastic referral to Naaman's wife, she, a child, was establishing a *stronghold* against God's enemy—a stronghold that silenced God's foe. Seemingly weak, she was powerful not in her own strength but in the power of the Holy Spirit.

The little slave girl was little more than a trophy to Naaman—a daily reminder of his victories. Yet it was out of this child's mouth that Naaman received the best news of his life. And Naaman listened to her. Though his faith right now was the size of a mustard seed, Naaman was beginning to believe. This was the great turning point in his life. All that follows in this story is a product of a simple testimony from a slave girl. Because of her simple testimony, Naaman was on the exciting path to healing, both physical and spiritual.

INVITATION TO JESUS

So this girl's character, her love, faithfulness, and goodness, all fruit of the Holy Spirit living in her, would prove to be the pivotal factors in the change about to come in Naaman's life. It would also be a great testimony to the power of Jehovah, Israel's God. But there is something more—something that towers "o'er the wrecks of time"[3]—in what she said. It is this: the slave girl's exclamation was an invitation to come to Jesus Christ.

We know this to be true because the statement is almost literally the testimony, the command, of the New Testament. It is the subsequent witness of the church and all Christians from that time on; it continues to be so today and will always be so to the end of the present age: *Would that you would go see the prophet in Israel! He would heal you!* This is the great gospel invitation to every man, woman, and child on the face of the earth. This is the healing that every person needs because everyone is terminal. David spoke of his own ravaging sickness because of sin:

> Because of your wrath there is no health in my body;
> there is no soundness in my bones because of
> my sin.
> My guilt has overwhelmed me
> like a burden too heavy to bear.
> My wounds fester and are loathsome
> because of my sinful folly.
> I am bowed down and brought very low;
> all day long I go about mourning.
> My back is filled with searing pain;
> there is no health in my body.
> I am feeble and utterly crushed;
> I groan in anguish of heart. (Ps. 38:3–8)

The slave girl didn't know about Jesus. But she did know about one of his predecessors, the prophet in Samaria, and she knew what he could do for someone who went to see him. Elisha represented Jesus, and she knew that he was exactly the one to see for a person who recognized that "there is no health in my body," who was feeble and utterly crushed, groaning in anguish of heart.

Elisha prefigured Jesus and was Jesus to this girl. He would become the same to Naaman. *Jesus* means "savior," or literally "the Lord is salvation." That is what this girl knew about Elisha. Naaman was looking right down the gun barrel as his life was being eaten away by leprosy.

The slave girl knew that, and she testified to what she knew: the prophet in Israel will save you. Jesus is the great healer.

Isaiah prophesies in the same way: "Surely he took up our pain, and bore our suffering" (Isa. 53:4a). "And by his wounds we are healed" (v. 5b). John Newton described his own need like this:

> Physician of my sin-sick soul,
> To thee I bring my case;
> My raging malady control,
> And heal me by thy grace.
>
> Pity the anguish I endure,
> See how I mourn and pine;
> For never can I hope a cure
> From any hand but thine.[4]

SHE PREACHED THE GOSPEL

This is the heart of the gospel, the good news that we preach. We are terminally ill, the walking dead. We are in desperate need of treatment that leads to life. There is only one place, only one person, where it can be found. All men and women need to hear that information from someone. This little slave girl was an ambassador from Israel, involuntarily so (like the apostle Paul in a Roman prison), but an ambassador nevertheless. She was a preacher—not the specific office that we recognize in the church today, but a *Preacher* with a capital *P*. She is a Preacher as described in Romans 10:14b–15: "How, then, can they call on the one they have not believed in? And how can they believe in the one of whom they have not heard? And how can they hear without someone preaching to them? And how can anyone preach unless they are sent? As it is written: 'How beautiful are the feet of those who bring good news!' "

Believers are preachers simply because they tell others about the gospel. They give this good news to others: there is a Prophet in Israel who will heal you! O that you would go meet with him! That is all a person needs to do. Recognize your need, admit your need, go see him, and he will heal you. This preaching is no vain effort, but guarantees results.

Though all believers are deemed preachers, maybe that is the ideal, and not the universal reality. Look at what this girl did. She proclaimed the gospel in unqualified terms to her enemy, to an avowed enemy of Israel. Most of us who profess to be Bible-believing Christians do not give the good news in that way. Certainly one reason is that we interpret being "on the battlefield for our Lord" to mean that we must show public opposition and even hostility to our spiritual enemies. For example, how do we characterize and treat people engaged in the abortion industry or terrorists? It is right for us to publicly denounce their acts as sin and offenses against a holy God, but do we also have the gospel heart to plead with such oppressed people to "go to Israel and get healed"? Do we have the humility to do this, and to enthusiastically and lovingly urge those hostile to the gospel to come to the Prophet in Israel? I am often far too timid, fearing an adverse response—or, worse, no response at all. I have the sense ahead of time that they won't believe what I say, so what's the use of saying it?

If there was ever anyone who could have felt that way, it was this little slave girl. Who would believe her? All she could reasonably expect in response was a good laugh. But if she had that fear, it did not deter her. I am rebuked by what she did. She shared the gospel joyfully and without concern as to the response.

So this slave told her master the incredibly good news. If he went to Samaria, he would be healed, and he would come to know Jehovah God of Israel. But as we will see later, she also unwittingly initiated a chain of events that would almost cost the Lord Jesus his life.

FOR FURTHER REFLECTION

1. Have you ever known anyone like this slave girl in that he or she was lonely, taken advantage of, abandoned, or abused? Has this ever been the case with you? If so, how did it feel?
2. Could this little girl have taken personal credit for her display of the fruit of the Spirit in her life?
3. In what ways did she "conform to the image of Christ"? (Look at Rom. 8:29.)
4. Do you ever have any reluctance, shame, or embarrassment in sharing your testimony? What causes it? What can be done to make a change?

CHAPTER FOUR

NAAMAN STEPS OUT

SURPRISING FAITH

Why did these Syrians believe this girl? She was only a slave child. She was hardly an obvious source for medical advice. A young child's best health-care tip often runs along these lines: "If I put a bandage on your face, your headache will get all better!" Loving, sweet, caring, and comforting—but unfortunately not accurate. We don't act on such counsel.

Yet Naaman's wife did not dismiss the girl's ebullient referral to the prophet in Samaria; she took it seriously enough to relay the message to her husband. Naaman did not dismiss it either. To the contrary, he went directly to his superior, the king of Aram, and told him what the slave girl had said. With seemingly no information other than what the girl had reported, Naaman immediately asked for permission to go to Israel and see this remarkable prophet who could heal him.

Why did they believe her? I think there are several reasons. First, the girl was obviously respected by Naaman's household. We don't know how long she had been a slave there, but during that time she had obviously gained a good reputation, much as Joseph did when he was a slave in Egypt, or as Daniel did as a captive in Babylon. Apparently, she was not a silly child, nor one given to tall tales.

Her word, even this seemingly outlandish word, had credibility. Her masters believed what she said that she knew.

Of course, Naaman was also at the end of his tether, and this condition will often pry the ear open a little. His health and his life were at stake, and he was desperately looking for an answer. He had to do something soon. And when people are in dire straits, they will often be willing to go out on a limb.

A member of our family had terminal cancer. All through his life, he had listened to no one but his doctor for medical direction. He was strictly a "you're the doctor" kind of guy. He was ultraconservative in this area and, among other things, rejected homeopathic remedies because his doctor opposed them. But after his doctor said that his cancer was incurable, he told me, "For all these years when my life was not at stake, I took my doctor's advice without questioning it. But now when I really need a doctor because my life *is* at stake, there's not a doctor alive who can help me!" So this otherwise commonsense, always-do-what-your-doctor-orders man decided to start looking at other possible remedies. He tried to figure out a way to get laetrile from Mexico, even though his doctors told him that it was false hope. He chopped up and ate peach and apricot pits. He was open to just about any remedy out there. Since the doctors couldn't help anyway, he realized that he might as well give such remedies a try. Can you blame him? No other cures were on the horizon.

This kind of desperation most likely played at least a part in Naaman's decision to follow the girl's advice. Nightmares are not necessarily evidence of a sleep disorder or psychological problems, but instead may be evidence of God's intervention, and are always under his sovereign control. He will use them to prod us in the direction he wants us to go.

I made reference earlier to a luncheon I attended where men gave their testimonies about how they had come to repentance and salvation. Almost all of them had had some terrible crisis in their lives that triggered their openness to the gospel. God not only uses such circumstances; he sovereignly initiates them to bring us to the end of ourselves in order to draw us to himself.

But ultimately, Naaman and his wife responded affirmatively to the girl's word because the Holy Spirit was at work in them as well as in her. That is a powerful combination, one that defies human wisdom. Even though Naaman was desperate, and even though they respected this girl, wasn't visiting a prophet in his enemy's country an utterly crazy idea? From a human standpoint, it was. So evidently there was another "standpoint" in this mix, an acceptance of her word initiated by the Lord himself.

Something else here confirms the idea that a force much more influential than mere worldly common sense was at work. Ben-Hadad, the king of Aram, also believed what the girl said! You would expect the king to figure that his top general had gone off his rocker, that the leprosy was affecting brain function. Yet the king not only confirmed Naaman's confidence in the girl, but did so enthusiastically. He immediately responded to Naaman, "By all means, go!—And I will send a letter with you to the king of Israel" (2 Kings 5:5).

Then Ben-Hadad put his money where his mouth was. He invested in the venture, backing it up with an enormous amount of money and property. The Aramean kingdom was banking—literally—on the hope that something good could come from his highly esteemed military commander's trip to Samaria, all based on what a young slave girl had said. Nothing else.

Also consider Naaman's servants, who accompanied the general on his trip. When Naaman initially refused to heed Elisha's commands and turned to head back to Damascus, his servants who were with him had the insight and courage to correct his path, urging him to do the *reasonable* thing and follow Elisha's instructions. So apparently quite a number of Syrians were convinced by the slave girl's words.

NAAMAN'S FAITH SHOWN BY ACTION

Naaman believed what he had heard. He was beginning to have faith. He took the girl at her word and immediately made plans to go on the journey. It wasn't complicated. He wasn't convinced by some complex or superior argument. He listened to the little girl as the Gentiles would listen to the apostle Paul: "When I came to you, I did not come with eloquence or human wisdom as I proclaimed to you the testimony about God. For I resolved to know nothing while I was with you except Jesus Christ and him crucified. I came to you in weakness with great fear and trembling. My message and my preaching were not with wise and persuasive words, but with a demonstration of the Spirit's power, so that your faith might not rest on human wisdom, but on God's power" (1 Cor. 2:1–5). Both the slave girl (the Preacher) and Naaman (the hearer) were engaged in a supernatural work. This work is far beyond human understanding. It was not human wisdom, but wisdom from above.

Naaman's "stepping out" was the faith of Abraham, to whom the Lord had said, "Go from your country and your kindred and your father's household to the land that I will show you. . . . *So Abram went*, as the Lord had told him" (Gen. 12:1–4). Similarly, Naaman, now beginning to be convinced of things not seen (Heb. 11:1), committed by action. Faith in God's word is true wisdom, and this kind of wisdom makes people do things that seem ridiculous to natural man apart from transformation by the Holy Spirit. But this is the brand of simple, straightforward, unquestioning faith in which God takes great joy.

It has always impressed me that the "faith hall of fame," the Hebrews 11 listing of Old Testament patriarchs and others whose faith God commends, contains no quotes from those commended. It is a chapter full of action, not verbal professions of faith, as important as those are (Rom. 10:9–10). Abraham *left* his hometown; Noah *built* the ark;

Abel *brought* the offering; Moses' parents *hid* their son; etc. Actions speak, testify, and teach powerfully. Though no word uttered by Abel appears in Scripture, yet "by faith Abel still *speaks*, even though he is dead" (Heb. 11:4). And although Naaman is not mentioned in Hebrews 11, he could be admitted to the same hall of fame because he *left*.

First, he prepared for the journey. Since he was the commander of Aram's armed forces, and because the king had sanctioned it, this would be an official trip. We aren't told how big his entourage was, but we do know how much money he took, and it was a whole lot. He put together 6,000 shekels of gold (150 pounds) and 10 talents of silver (750 pounds). At this writing, gold is valued at $1,492 an ounce, and silver is selling for about $34 an ounce. So Naaman was carrying what today would be worth $3,580,800 in gold and $408,000 in silver. The total cash amount would have been just shy of $4 million in today's market. Throwing in the "ten sets of clothing" (which had considerable value in that day) and allowing for the ups and downs of the precious-metals market, we'll round it off at $4 million.

It would appear that high medical costs are nothing new. The little girl's referral was getting to be expensive. Naaman and his king assumed that a healing like this—if it were to be successful—would of course be costly, but to them it would be worth every shekel. There is no free lunch, and there certainly is no free medical treatment, especially in a country deemed your enemy.

BEN-HADAD'S LETTER

Naaman also went armed with a letter from the king of Aram. Chain of command is evident in this story. Since Naaman was answerable to his king, he assumed that the proper way to contact the storied "prophet in Samaria" would be by first visiting the king of Israel. On a diagram it would be Naaman up to Syrian king, king reaching sideways to king, king down to prophet. Naaman needed to make his approach to Israel in compliance with the diplomatic protocol of the day.

Therefore, it was necessary to come armed with Ben-Hadad's letter to Jehoram, the king of Israel, and bring the massive amount of money, especially since a hostile relationship existed between Aram and Israel. Even assuming that the two countries were honoring some kind of temporary truce at the time, it had to be an uneasy one, for the Bible speaks of open hostilities between the countries both before and after this event. Naaman could not go empty-handed. And even during a cold war, money talks.

We are given the text of the brief letter that Ben-Hadad sent to the king of Israel: "With this letter I am sending my servant Naaman to you so that you may cure him of his leprosy" (2 Kings 5:6). It is not likely that the king of Aram believed that Israel's king was himself the prophet. Rather, he was following the chain of command, directing the letter and the request to the king of Israel because he assumed that any prophet in Israel capable of performing such a healing would be a valuable asset to the kingdom and therefore under the king's authority. Thus Ben-Hadad must have thought it was safe to assume that Israel's king, by giving his command, would summon the prophet and delegate him to perform the healing ceremony.

JEHORAM'S UNGODLY RESPONSE

But when the king of Israel read the letter, he flew into a rage. He ripped his clothes. "Am I God? Can I kill and bring back to life? Why does this fellow send someone to me to be cured of his leprosy? See how he is trying to pick a quarrel with me!" (2 Kings 5:7).

It is possible that King Jehoram didn't know much about Elisha, but that isn't likely, because the Lord had previously displayed his miraculous powers several times through Elisha. After Elijah was whisked away to heaven in a whirlwind, Elisha had received a "double portion" of his master's spirit, and he took Elijah's cloak and parted the waters of the Jordan River so that he could cross over (2 Kings 2:9–14). He healed the waters of the city of Jericho (2:19–22), and on his way to Bethel, when a gang of boys jeered him, he sent bears to attack the boys (2:23–24). He cured a poisonous pot of stew (4:38–44). He caused oil to flow for a widow, so that she could fill all the containers she could find, sell the oil, pay her debts, and have enough left over to live on (4:1–7). He promised a wealthy but barren woman from Shunem that she would conceive and give birth to a son, which she did (4:11–17). After her boy had grown, he died while working in the hot sun. In perhaps his most dazzling display of the Lord's power resident in him, Elisha raised the boy from the dead (4:18–37).

A particular one of these displays of miraculous power must have been well known to King Jehoram. Elisha had miraculously brought streams and pools of water to aid Israel, Judah, and Edom, which had formed a dubious alliance to battle the Moabites—both to give Israel's fighting men something to drink and then to lure the Moabites into a fatal ambush. The Moabites mistook the red reflection of morning sun on the water for blood, and assumed that the three kings had "fought and slaughtered each other" (2 Kings 3:13–27). As the Moabites charged headlong to take the spoils, Israel was waiting in ambush and soundly defeated them.

It stretches believability to assume, then, that Jehoram didn't know about at least some of these recorded miracles. The most likely reason the king didn't send Naaman to Elisha was that he did not believe Elisha could cure him. Jehoram did not have faith. It was the same in Jesus' generation. Even though his miracles were many and well documented, they did not cause most people to believe. In fact, it was exactly because of his miracles that they wanted to kill him (John 12:10–11).

Since Jehoram didn't believe Elisha could cure Naaman, all he could figure was that Ben-Hadad was trying to set him up for a fight—sending him a demand that he knew couldn't possibly be met! In the early stages of World War II, Hitler sent demand after demand to Poland for the purpose of manufacturing an excuse for an invasion when Poland did not comply. Hitler wanted to pick a fight. Similarly, the king of Israel believed that this request for Naaman's healing was a ploy, a pretense aimed at giving Aram an excuse to battle Israel once again: issue an impossible demand to justify the unjustifiable.

Jehoram's problem was that he did not see the world as being God's world. When he encountered such a crisis, he refused to consider what the Lord might be doing. He evaluated it only in human terms. His encounter with Naaman was not the only time he did so. Two chapters later, when the Syrians surrounded and besieged starving Samaria, one night the Lord stepped in and caused the entire Syrian army to flee, leaving all their belongings and food behind. Four lepers went out to investigate and brought the good news back to the king. Jehoram's response is recorded:

> And the king rose in the night and said to his servants, "I will tell you what the Syrians have done to us. They know that we are hungry. Therefore they have gone out of the camp to hide themselves in the open country, thinking, 'When they come out of the city, we shall take them alive and get into the city.'" (2 Kings 7:12 ESV)

KEEPING GOD IN THE PICTURE

We commit serious error when we remove God from the picture. Jehoram had witnessed plenty of God's miraculous interventions in Israel, but he stubbornly refused to believe. In each of these cases, Jehoram's lack of faith resulted in suspicion and fear. In the throne room, after Naaman's visit, he tore his clothes and feared that Ben-Hadad was looking for a reason to fight. When the Syrians mysteriously disappeared, Jehoram could not accept that God had miraculously provided for Israel's starving people, but instead suspected trickery and coming defeat. The king of Israel did not believe; Naaman the Syrian did.

Compare Jehoram's reactions to King David's in similar situations. When Jehoram faced a challenge, he threw up his hands. But even as a youth, David met the challenge, broadcasting to the world where he was looking for help. "You come against me with sword and spear and javelin, but I come against you in the name of the LORD Almighty, the God of the armies of Israel, whom you have defied!" he shouted out to Goliath the giant (1 Sam. 17:45). David did not tear his clothes or throw up his hands; instead, he reveled in the opportunity to proclaim the name of the Lord.

We should tear our garments or wear sackcloth and ashes as we fall down before the Lord and seek his mercy, not when throwing up our hands in desperation before men. In the story of Jonah, when he preached of God's imminent judgment on the Ninevites, the more than a hundred thousand citizens of the city, even the pagan mayor, saw what needed to be done. The mayor then issued this decree:

> "Do not let people or animals, herds or flocks, taste anything; do not let them eat or drink. But let people and animals be covered with sackcloth. Let everyone call urgently on God. Let them give up their evil ways and their violence. Who knows? God may yet relent and with compassion turn from his fierce anger so that we will not perish."
>
> When God saw what they did and how they turned from their evil ways, he relented and did not bring on them the destruction he had threatened. (Jonah 3:7–10)

When wicked King Ahab, after Elijah pronounced God's judgment on him for his sin in leading Israel astray, "tore his clothes, put on sackcloth and fasted," God responded with overwhelming mercy:

> Then the word of the LORD came to Elijah the Tishbite: "Have you noticed how Ahab has humbled himself before me? Because he has humbled himself, I will not bring this disaster in his day, but I will bring it on his house in the days of his son." (1 Kings 21:27–29)

Because Ahab humbled himself *before the Lord*, not men, God relented and delayed judgment until after Ahab's death. By contrast, when Naaman showed up, Ahab's son Jehoram didn't even think of the Lord in this predicament; instead, he humbled himself before the Syrian delegation. In this respect, he was even worse than his dad, and that was no small accomplishment.

PROPHET WITHOUT HONOR

So look at the "upside-downness" of the situation. Naaman and his king—heathen Gentiles—thought that a prophet in Israel could heal Naaman of his leprosy. They had more faith than the king of Israel did! The Jewish prophet was being honored more in Damascus than in Israel. But this "upside-downness" is inimical to the human race, and should come as no great surprise. "A prophet is not without honor except in his own town and in his own home," Jesus told the people in his hometown of Nazareth (Matt. 13:57). Thus Jesus "did not do many miracles there because of their lack of faith" (13:58).

"Who has believed our message and to whom has the arm of the LORD been revealed?" (Isa. 53:1). Not Jehoram the king of Israel. He didn't believe Naaman's report, and he didn't believe the lepers' report. He did not allow the arm of the Lord to be revealed to him or anyone else. He should have believed. Though the kingdom was divided at this time, this king sat on Israel's throne. He should have been like Moses, Joshua, Samuel, and David.

But Naaman was not standing before Jehoram, letter in hand, to pick a fight. He was there to get healed. He was in the right place—a place where he should have been able to hear the good news of God's healing power. He was standing before the king of God's chosen people. But it had begun to look like he had come to the wrong place.

When Jehoram responded this way, Naaman surely must have worried that his trip had been in vain. He might have begun to doubt the words of his slave girl. If the king of Israel didn't know about this prophet, who would? Had he been sent on a buggy ride? Should he just turn around and go home, recognizing that this kind of thing couldn't be for real anyway? Would he be the laughingstock of Damascus when he returned home as leprous as when he left? Would he become the village idiot for believing his slave girl's tall tale? Naaman must have thought, if only for an instant, that he might be chasing an embarrassing rainbow.

IRRESISTIBLE GRACE

But "he who began a good work in you will carry it on to completion" (Phil. 1:6), so this venture was still on track, no matter what it looked like here in the palace. John Calvin spoke of God's "irresistible grace," and Naaman was finding out what that means. God finishes what he starts. Furthermore, there was divine purpose in this failed stop with the king in Samaria.

The work that was about to be accomplished in Naaman's life would not be the product of a king's power or human authority. Naaman was accustomed to having important things accomplished through the chain of command. This healing trip, he would discover, was quite different. The king of Israel could not employ or delegate the power of God. Jehoram was at least right when he protested, "Am I God? Can I kill and make alive?" Of course not. God's servant Elisha was Israel's great prophet, and he did not answer to the king of Israel or to any other human authority. Through this encounter with the king, Naaman was beginning to understand that what was about to happen to him was going to be entirely outside the human chain of command.

FOR FURTHER REFLECTION

1. What caused Naaman's wife, Naaman, and Ben-Hadad to trust what the slave girl said? What gave her testimony credibility?
2. Have you ever been in a serious predicament with no way out? Did this cause you to look to sources of help that you had not previously considered?
3. When you were forced to look for help, what were your motives and priorities? Were you looking at just human, or earthly, objectives? Did you consider what the Lord's objectives for you might be in the situation?
4. How did Jehoram's outburst help Naaman in Naaman's understanding of what was about to happen to him?
5. What evidence of the work of reconciliation, if any, do you see in the relationship of the little slave girl and Naaman?

CHAPTER FIVE

ELISHA, PART 1

THE PROPHET INTERVENES

The prophet got wind of what was happening at the palace. Exactly how he found out we are not told, but it was pretty difficult to keep secrets from Elisha (see 2 Kings 5:26). He knew what had transpired—that the king had ripped his clothes because of Naaman's request—and he sent Jehoram a message: "Why have you torn your robes? Have the man come to me and he will know that there is a prophet in Israel" (v. 8). Elisha was embarrassed for Israel because of the king's actions, and I think also for the God of Israel.

What Elisha sent to the king was not just a message. It was a severe rebuke. Jehoram should have known that there was a prophet in Israel who could heal Naaman. He was the ruler of God's chosen people and should have known about the miracles that Elisha had already performed. But the king did not believe, and in refusing to acknowledge Elisha as the man of God, he was in fact refusing to acknowledge God himself. The king was demonstrating in a public forum that he did not believe a supernatural God was at work in Israel. Tearing his clothes off and accusing the king of Aram of trying to "pick a fight" showed that the king of Israel was interpreting events in a godless way, giving the lie to the power of the true God.

Elisha did not say, "Have the man come to me and I will heal him." That was going to happen, but Elisha's prime goal was to teach Naaman that there was a prophet in Israel. And through the prophet, Naaman would meet the God of Israel, which was what it was all about. There is no doubt that Naaman would be thankful if he were healed. But Elisha was looking at the big picture, and he wanted Naaman to be giving infinitely more thanks for being led to the one living and true God. So when Elisha says, "Have the man come to me and he will know that there is a prophet in Israel," he doesn't mention healing because he is speaking to Naaman's ultimate and real need, which Naaman later goes on record as understanding.

A MEETING ON THE LAWN

When Naaman heard the invitation from the messenger, he was out the palace door in a flash, heading immediately to Elisha's residence. "Naaman came with his horses and chariots and stood at the door of Elisha's house" (2 Kings 5:9). He went with his entourage, loaded with gold and silver for Elisha, ready to do business with Israel's heralded prophet. But when he got there and announced his arrival, Elisha was otherwise occupied—perhaps taking a phone call, catching up on his e-mail, or dictating a letter—and couldn't come to the door. Instead, Elisha sent one of his servants, who instructed Naaman to "go and wash in the Jordan seven times, and your flesh shall be restored, and you shall be clean" (v. 10).

This had to be quite a scene. A royal entourage parked in front of the prophet's residence—likely the most ostentatious set of visitors that Elisha had ever had. This was the delegation from Aram that had just gained audience with the king of Israel. Now Naaman had, upon invitation, come to the prophet's home, and of course wanted and expected to meet Elisha. But Elisha didn't show. Rather, he sent his servant to the door, with instructions to direct Naaman to wash in the Jordan. There was no need for Naaman to see the prophet personally.

NAAMAN'S TANTRUM

But this treatment did not go over well with Naaman. He was angry—so angry that he turned to leave and go back home. He did not expect this kind of response, or nonresponse. He didn't expect Elisha to ignore him in any respect. He assumed that the prophet would diplomatically meet and greet him in a manner befitting a foreign chief of staff. Naaman was an important man and expected to be treated accordingly. He wanted a royal welcome, a ceremony, an incantation. He wanted a "photo op."

Naaman tells his men explicitly why he is so upset: "I thought that he would surely come out to me and stand and call upon the name of the LORD his God and wave his hand over the place and cure the leper" (2 Kings 5:11).

This is what Naaman had envisioned. On his trip from Damascus to Samaria, he had conjured up a picture of what this healing event would look like, and it sure wasn't slithering like a frog into the dirty Jordan River seven times, without the prophet's even being there to preside over the event. He was picturing a high ceremony, a hocus-pocus incantation during which Elisha called on his God (not Naaman's god), a wave of the prophet's hand, and shazam! Healed! He had figured that this would be a fairy-godmother event, as when Cinderella was transformed on the night of the royal ball. Naaman wanted something special, something magical. Anything less would hurt his pride.

Pride is called *deadly* with good reason. For me, and I suspect for many others, it seems virtually unconquerable. It takes countless forms. In my case, it often evidences itself not so much in obvious braggadocio or arrogance but in more sinister ways, such as causing me to think I can pretty much dictate the events in my life. I turn to myself.

And it always ends in failure. But no problem—like a fool, I do the same thing next time. Pride, no matter what form it takes, blinds us to reality and thus makes us act stupidly. In the natural state, Luther said, "sin had made me crazy,"[1] and he was not exaggerating.

That happened to Naaman, at least momentarily. As he left Elisha's house, pride threatened to get the best of him, blocking his path and thwarting his own best interest. Vanity was skewing his priorities, blinding him from the reality of his plight and thus threatening a potential remedy. Conceit was about to keep him from the very thing he needed the most. He had leprosy. That was why he was here standing in front of Elisha's house. He needed healing,* not a ceremonial incantation.

But Naaman lost sight of what he needed the most when he heard Elisha's message. It was bad enough that Elisha didn't come out to perform the healing personally. On top of that, the prophet wanted the Syrian general to go dip himself in the Jordan River, which to this day has a reputation for carrying a considerable amount of sediment. The Jordan is known as a dirty river. If dipping myself in water is what it takes to heal me, Naaman thought angrily, at least I ought to be able to choose a decent river. Sparkling clean water, such as what flowed in the Damascus rivers Abana and Pharpar, would be far preferable, and the risk of infection (particularly due to his open sores) would be lessened in that crystal-clear water. Further, Naaman reasoned that if he had known that dipping himself in water would heal, he could have avoided this expensive trip!

SALVATION IS NOT ON OUR TERMS

But Naaman was not directing this event. Elisha the prophet, speaking and acting for the Lord, was in charge. Elisha knew that Naaman could not come to this on his own terms. Naaman might have thought that the best and proper way to conduct this healing was for him and Elisha to stand through the ceremony in a royal and respectable way in a river of Naaman's choice. But Elisha had commanded Naaman to make a trip to a dirty river in his enemy's land, get down on his hands and knees, and soak himself head to foot in that muddy water. Not just once, but seven times.

When he received Elisha's message, Naaman started thinking as a natural man, as Jehoram (who should have known better) had done back at the palace. We could expect little else. Since Elisha was not going to attend, Naaman assumed that it would be the water that healed him. He did not yet grasp the fact that the power was not in the water, but in Jehovah God. The power to heal was not in Elisha, either, though he was the Lord's agent for bringing about the healing. Both the water of the Jordan and the prophet would be used in the healing. Jesus used saliva and mud to heal the blind. But the power is always from the Lord.

We human beings are all like Naaman. We want ceremony, formality, a "falling down before the Lord" in our brains only, but not as the apostle John witnessed on the isle of Patmos, where "all the angels were standing around the throne and around the elders and the four living creatures, and they fell on their faces before the throne and worshiped God" (Rev. 7:11). We should beware of ceremony. It can easily obscure the fact that healing comes as we bend the knee.

It is hard enough to bend the knee, but to fall on your face? Mud made from saliva and dirt? The dirty Jordan? These methods are degrading, and we think unnecessary.

But it is never on our terms that the Lord heals us—physically or spiritually. We do not enter the kingdom of heaven standing tall, full of ourselves, directing events. It is always on our knees, when we come to the end of ourselves, of doing things our own way. It is not intended to be easy. We want to be the copilot and often the pilot, but salvation is altogether God's domain.

Recall that the Arameans were used to manipulating their gods. That was their view of divine beings. Their gods had limited sovereignty—limited by their peculiar specializations and geographical boundaries. Gods must be kept in their place.

Naaman was not used to dealing with the God who called all the shots, who was sovereign over everything and everyone. He wanted to be at least partly in control. Like Frank Sinatra's vapid (and satanic) song "My Way," in which he claims that he did not live his life as one who kneels, but that he did it "my way."[2]

This is precisely the position that Satan has taken before the Lord. And as "Old Blue Eyes" sang, this is what the record shows. Can you imagine anything more self-damning? From the time the devil rebelled in heaven, he has been doing his own thing. He decided not to submit. He determined to do it his way. He chose to begin "saying the things he truly feels and not the words of one who kneels." Because he refused to bow before his Maker, King of kings and Lord of lords, he was cast from heaven like lightning.

But we must be humble in this deadly serious matter. What does the "record show" in my life? I may not sing along with Sinatra, but self-examination shows that maybe Sinatra was bold enough to speak—or sing—the sad truth that I shrink from. In fact, all of us have a self-damning record because of our determination to do things our way. This is why we cry out for the only cure, "God, be merciful to me, a sinner!" (Luke 18:13). The awful record can be cleared. What a phenomenal gospel!

It's worth noting that this is the first time in the story that Naaman starts to turn aside from his mission. He had listened to his wife. He had believed the little slave girl. He had such hope and confidence that the prophet in Israel could heal him that he rushed to his king to get permission to go. He put together a fortune to pay for it, assembled his troupe, took the trip, and put up with outright resistance from the king of Israel when he got to Samaria. But his silly, dangerous vanity was ready to throw all that effort and all his hope into the trash can. I'd like to say that his temper tantrum and raging, impulsive decision to return to Damascus is unbelievable, but my mouth is stopped. I have so often done exactly the same thing. Pride blinds. We forfeit everything when we let it get the upper hand.

Naaman was not the first human being to try it his way. Cain tried, too. He brought God a sacrifice different from what the Lord had commanded, and God would not accept it. His brother Abel's sacrifice was accepted because it was what God had prescribed. And when God rejected his offering, Cain, just like Naaman, lost his temper. Then the Lord confronted Cain, asking him, "Why are you angry? Why is your face downcast? If you do what is right, will you not be accepted? But if you do not do what is right, sin is crouching at your door; it desires to have you, but you must rule over it" (Gen. 4:6–7).

Like Cain, Naaman was acting like a crazy man. He was turning back on the road to Damascus, abandoning his whole mission. This happens when temper takes over. A person gets furious and rashly decides to dump the whole thing. In Naaman's case, it was "my way or the highway"—literally.

NAAMAN'S SERVANTS INTERVENE

It's providential that Naaman brought his servants. The Syrian general was accustomed to giving orders to his men, and they were accustomed to taking them. But in this case, his servants ventured a respectful but strong rebuke, hoping to bring him to his senses. They collared him, asking, "My father, if the prophet had told you to do some great thing, would you not have done it? How much more, then, when he tells you, 'Wash and be cleansed'!" (2 Kings 5:13).

Naaman would not have been upset if Elisha had directed him to do a "great thing," something like a pilgrimage, a penance, walking on hot coals—something sensational, flashy, and brave, like going on an adventurous quest for the Holy Grail. But Elisha prescribed something humiliating and undignified, something that Naaman felt was degrading. He did not want to do this kind of thing, particularly in front of his men.

In their anger, Cain and Naaman stood at the same fork in the road. They could yield to the Lord and humble themselves, or they could insist on their own way. There is no question that God gave Cain a way out—"if you do what is right, you will be accepted." But Cain gave in to his anger and went where it took him. Naaman listened to wise voices. We know from comparing the two events what an enormous difference can come from what might seem to be a relatively benign choice. For the one who insisted on going his own way, the end was murder. But for the man who listened, it meant acceptance, healing, and eternal salvation.

Naaman listened to his servants twice in this story: first when he listened to his slave girl, and then when he listened to his troops. Listening to and heeding the pleas of servants took humility. Somehow his heart had softened to the point that he could hear others, even those he considered inferior to him. Both times, when Naaman accepted their counsel, his path was cleared to God's blessing.

FOR FURTHER REFLECTION

1. What was Elisha's primary objective in inviting Naaman to come to his home? Why do you think that was his reason?

2. What were some of the reasons that Elisha ordered Naaman to go to the Jordan River rather than accepting Naaman's plans? What does this say

about preparation of the heart in order to bring about reconciliation?

3. Why is it important for us not to bravely try things our way? Why does the Lord not honor that effort?

4. Is there any lesson to be learned from the fact that Naaman listened to his servants, his inferiors? What does this say about the process of healing, salvation, and reconciliation?

CHAPTER SIX

HEALED

INTO THE RIVER

A trip to the Jordan River from the city of Samaria is somewhere around twenty-five to thirty-five miles, depending on the route taken. So it likely took Naaman and his troupe a couple of days to make the round trip. The Scripture says only that "he went down and dipped himself in the Jordan" (2 Kings 5:14), but gives no more details of the trip. You can't tell what Naaman's state of mind was, but given the fact that he had lost his temper because Elisha directed that he wash in the Jordan, it wouldn't be surprising if he were still somewhat pouty and reluctant, just having submitted to the advice of his men. And it follows that he must have had some misgivings about the whole venture. It is doubtful that he was the one out front, leading the charge. Still, he went.

When he got to the muddy Jordan, Naaman dipped himself in the river seven times, as Elisha had prescribed. And he was healed of his leprosy, just as his little slave girl and the prophet had foretold. He came up out of the river after the seventh dip, and his flesh was restored and became "clean like that of a young boy" (2 Kings 5:14).

What a sight. The general comes in his chariot, with all his attendants, gold, silver, and expensive clothing. He has the official letter in hand from his king directing that the king of Israel heal him. The company halts near the riverbank, with all that in tow. But Naaman must leave all that behind him as he goes down into the Jordan. He even must remove his robe. He has to strip down to his underwear for this procedure. He couldn't carry any of the official dictates, protocol, riches, fancy clothing, or ideas of high-sounding ceremony with him. Just his body, immersed in the Jordan. Nothing but simple, unadorned obedience: "as the man of God had told him" (2 Kings 5:14).

God told Abraham to get out of Ur of the Chaldees; Abraham did it. Elisha told Naaman to dip seven times in the Jordan; Naaman did it.

JESUS ACCOMPANIED NAAMAN

And when Naaman went down into the river, he was accompanied by another: Jesus himself. He led Naaman in this simple, humble act. He led by his presence and example. He is the One who, "being in very nature God, did not consider equality with God something to be used to his own advantage; rather, he made himself nothing by taking the very nature of a servant, being made in human likeness. And being found in appearance as a man, he humbled himself by becoming obedient to death—even death on a cross" (Phil. 2:6–8). Jesus does not follow us in *our* humility, but we follow him in *his*. There is no other path to the Lord's blessing, no other hope for cure.

Jesus emptied himself of his glory when he came into the world. He put that aside so that he could save sinful man. All accoutrements of office, the outward signs of his absolute authority over everything and everyone in the universe—those things he left behind. Thus he could help Naaman leave the accoutrements of his position and power, too, back on the riverbank. Those things had no part in salvation. Those things were of no use here. Jesus was entering the Jordan with Naaman. There was no way for Naaman, nor is there any way for one of us, to enter the kingdom of heaven with all those things weighing us down.

There was also no way for Naaman, nor is there for any of us, to enter the kingdom but on his knees. Thus the Lord brought Naaman down to his knees and humbled him. God humbled Naaman but did not humiliate him. A friend of mine who recently exited the hospital after a week or so told me that in the hospital he felt he had lost his modesty—but not his dignity. Thus it is with us when God brings us to salvation. We are brought to humble submission, but not utterly shamed. Naaman's sevenfold immersion, particularly in front of his attendants, was humbling, but it turned out not to be demeaning.

BORN AGAIN

Naaman came up joyfully out of the river with a new and healthy body, sporting flesh like that of a young boy. For his men, this would take some getting used to—getting accustomed to looking at their general with skin that looked like a young boy's! Their formerly battle-worn leader now looked like a child in an adult's body. What would it be like to be under the command of someone who looked like he was going through puberty? One thing we know: this physical change in Naaman would be a constant reminder not only to him, but also to his men and everyone else who knew him, that on that day in the Jordan, at the command of the man of God, something supernatural had happened. Naaman was transformed in this life and forever, and it was obvious to the eye.

I am seventy, and my wife is nipping at my heels. We have four grandchildren, ages sixteen down to six. If you are, say, fifty or older, I'm sure that like me you have looked at the skin of such young children and yearned for the day long ago when your skin looked like that. Their arms are smooth and clear—no wrinkles or age spots. Their necks do not sag, and their skin is smooth, firm, and well toned. Sometimes we yearn to turn back the clock, if only to have skin like a child.

That was the gift that Naaman received. The leprosy was gone, but he got more than that. Naaman's age is not disclosed in Scripture, but he was an adult with leprosy, which meant that he had numerous lesions and open sores. When a festering disease like this is arrested and cured, the open sores scab over as the healing process progresses, leaving visible scarring—a solemn reminder of the former disease. But Naaman had no scars. His flesh was restored like that of a young boy! The horrible lesions were all gone, in an instant. He was clean, cured in a moment. As knowledge of what had happened to his body began to sink in, it's safe to say that Naaman also began to experience the kind of unbridled joy that a kid exhibits.

When Nicodemus came to Jesus by night (John 3), Jesus told him that "no one can see the kingdom of God unless they are born again." "How can someone be born when they are old?" Nicodemus asked. "Surely they cannot enter a second time into their mother's womb to be born!"

Obviously not. Jesus was talking about spiritual rebirth, not physical. But Naaman was brought closer than anyone else to actual physical rebirth. He didn't go all the way back to his mother's womb, but God took him back pretty far—back to the "young boy" stage. In this instance, the Jordan was truly a fountain of youth.

Can you imagine how Naaman felt? He looked not just once but dozens of times at his arms and legs. He had to pinch that new skin to assure himself that this was not a dream. Had anyone ever heard of such a thing? There must have been some un-military-like high fives between Naaman and his men, cavorting and shouting in astonishment and unmitigated joy.

His mind must also have turned to his little Jewish slave girl. He could remember her cheerful voice, her simple, unflinching confidence in the prophet in Israel.

Now her outlandish assurance had been confirmed. Naaman had to be thinking of her, what he would say when he returned to Damascus, and how he could adequately thank and reward her for what she had done. His skin was now like hers! Words would not be sufficient. Nothing he could imagine would be adequate. How had she known that this would happen? A child was responsible for his miraculous healing!

NAAMAN TRANSFORMED FOREVER

What the slave girl's faithful and kind word had brought about was much more than a medical miracle. Naaman was changed forever. It may have started in his body, but it moved quickly into his heart and soul. If he had known the lyrics, he would have been singing this spiritual:

I know I've been changed
I know I've been changed
I know I've been changed
The angels in Heaven done signed my name.

Well if you don't believe that I've been redeemed
Oh follow me down to that old Jordan stream
I stepped in the water and the water was cold
Oh it chilled my body but not my soul.
The angels in Heaven done signed my name.[1]

The servants, watching this miracle from the riverbank, must have been shocked out of *their* skin. Even though they were the ones who had urged Naaman to do what the prophet said, their eyes surely were like saucers when the healing actually happened. They probably were like Rhoda in Acts 12, the servant girl who was praying with other Christians for Peter's release from prison. By all rights she should have been expecting a miracle, and when she heard a knock at the door and answered it, she actually saw Peter standing there! She was so amazed and overjoyed that she ran back inside to tell the house church what had happened without unlocking the door, leaving poor Peter still standing there. Expecting it? Kind of. But still incredulous. Any Christian who has had prayer answered in a specific way knows exactly what Rhoda went through. We pray and pray and pray for God to do something. We even believe, at least theoretically, that it can happen. Then we see that our specific prayer is specifically answered, and we can scarcely believe it. It's astounding and too good to be true.

Naaman could have made a beeline to Damascus after the healing in the Jordan, but that would have been disrespectful to Elisha, and ungrateful, too. Moreover, it wasn't what he wanted to do. What he wanted was to go back to Samaria. He had to share this incredible news with Elisha. He had to express his gratitude for this amazing cure.

FOR FURTHER REFLECTION

1. What evidence is there in this story or from other Scripture that the Lord himself was with Naaman while he was being healed?
2. What significance is there in the fact that Naaman's diseased flesh was restored to that of a young boy?
3. Why did Naaman want to go by Elisha's home on his way back to Damascus?
4. What does Naaman's grateful spirit say about what had just happened to him? Contrast this with the response of the ten lepers whose healing was recorded in Luke 17:11–19.
5. Why is a thankful spirit a high priority to the Lord?

CHAPTER SEVEN

ELISHA, PART 2

NEWS TO SHARE

Naaman had great news to share with everybody, but the one he particularly wanted to see right now was Elisha. Naaman wanted to show the great prophet his healed body, to thank him, and to give him a thank-you present. First, though, came his testimony. When he got back to Elisha's residence, Naaman exclaimed: "Now I know that there is no God in all the world except in Israel" (2 Kings 5:15). It is significant that this confession of faith came before any other recorded word. Naaman had this at the top of his list, even ahead of his physical healing. The awareness of the fact that "there is no God in all the world except in Israel" dominated his thinking.

Remember when Elisha sent messengers to Jehoram, after the king had torn off his clothes in exasperation and anger? Elisha didn't say, "Have the man come to me so he will know that I can heal him," but "so that he will know that there is a prophet in Israel" (2 Kings 5:8). Here was Naaman—fresh back from being healed, cleansed from his leprosy—and he exclaimed, "Now I know that there is no God in all the world except in Israel." This was the very outcome that Elisha desired and anticipated. It had been accomplished.

ISRAEL'S GOD THE ONLY GOD

Step back a bit and take a look at what momentous changes had taken place in Naaman already, as evidenced by this great confession. Recall once more what the Aramean military had concluded after the unsuccessful battle with Israel recorded in 1 Kings 20. Naaman's military thought they had figured out Israel's God: "Their gods are gods of the hills, and so they were stronger than we." As mentioned in chapter 2, they believed that all gods were limited and parochial, including Israel's God. But they were mistaken. And to this day, no one has figured out or contained Jehovah God.

Naaman's world had been turned upside down. "This is amazing!" he must have thought. "There is no God in all the world except in Israel. That covers a whole lot of ground! It means that he is the God of everything. It covers not only Israel but Aram, Damascus, Illinois, Reno, and everyone and everything else in the universe. Those gods that I used to worship, and those I didn't—none of them are gods at all!" Naaman could have responded, "Now I know that in addition to being the god of the hills, Israel's god is also the god of healing leprosy. This god has at least two specialties." But something far more profound had happened to Naaman. He had come to know a God who is "infinite, eternal, and unchangeable."[1] This is the One in whom he was already beginning to live and move and have his being (Acts 17:28). Naaman had been transformed by the gospel.

In Naaman's exclamation we can see something of the nature of the Holy Spirit's work in a person when this transformation occurs. Sometimes these things are immediate. Naaman immediately saw who was truly responsible for the healing he had just experienced. He did not mention his slave girl's part in it, or even Elisha's. Instantly, and in his new nature instinctively, he knew that it was the God of Israel. No one needed to tell him that, because the Holy Spirit had already written that truth indelibly on his mind and heart.

Naaman had *saving* faith; he was a *believer.* He now knew the Jehovah God of Israel, though he had not yet filled in all the blanks, and though he had not seen him, he had become certain of what he did not see (Heb. 11:1). Naaman had joined those of us who share in the faith of Abraham, whose faith was "credited to him as righteousness" (Gen. 15:6; Rom. 4:3, 22). Naaman, through this momentous transaction, had been made righteous before God.

It is significant that in Naaman's exchange with Elisha, neither he nor Elisha mentioned the healing. The miracle, as is true of all miracles, was a powerful, convincing sign and certainly worthy of mention. But even though it was of momentous importance to Naaman and his future, the healing of his body was a distant second to the healing that had taken place in his heart. Naaman already had his testimony etched in his mind, being overwhelmed with his new acquaintance with the true God. So it was with the man born blind, whom Jesus healed, recorded in John 9:

> Jesus heard that they had thrown him [the man born blind] out [of the synagogue], and when he found him, he said, "Do you believe in the Son of Man?" "Who is he, sir?" the man asked. "Tell me so that I may believe in him." Jesus said, "You have now seen him; in fact, he is the one speaking with you." Then the man said, "Lord, I believe," *and he worshiped him.* (John 9:35–38)

The miracle of healing is corollary to the more important event: the implanting of faith in a new believer.

NAAMAN WANTS TO PAY

It is not surprising that Naaman was very, very appreciative of what Elisha had done. He looked back at his chariot and wagons, saw all the money and Brooks Brothers clothing he had brought, and made a request of Elisha: "So please accept a gift from your servant" (2 Kings 5:15). This was not an evil request. He was not like Simon the sorcerer in Acts 8, who tried to purchase the healing power of the Holy Spirit so that he could profit from it in his business. What Naaman wanted to do was to show his gratitude in a meaningful way. He did not want to be a cheapskate when Elisha's God had bestowed on him such great favor.

It may seem insignificant, but Naaman did not use the words "accept compensation" from your servant, or "I truly want to pay you something for your services," but "accept a gift." He must have realized that no amount of money or clothing could come close to being adequate payment for what he had received. His healing, and especially his vastly changed worldview—"now I know that there is no God in all the world except in Israel"—were beyond an earthly price tag. He recognized that immediately, so he did not cheapen the event by making an offer. He simply conveyed a desire to make a gift to the pastor and his parish.

ELISHA DECLINES NAAMAN'S OFFER

Elisha's immediate response shocked Naaman and his attendants: "As surely as the LORD lives, whom I serve, I will not accept a thing" (2 Kings 5:16). Of course, Elisha, though the prophet of the God of Israel, was human and subject to human temptation. He must have been tempted by this offer, especially coming from the very man who had waged war against Israel. Couldn't it be reasonably considered a partial reparation for war crimes of Aram against Israel, crimes such as capturing and enslaving little girls? It could be characterized as a great blessing from God himself. I mean, just look at the amazing way in which God works to bring blessing to his people! You could even say that this influx of money into Elisha's ministry was God's way of confirming obedience. There were dozens of ways in which Elisha could have justified taking the money and issuing a receipt for tax purposes.

But Elisha refused, and his refusal did not come out of the goodness of his heart. He did not say, "That's awfully nice of you, Naaman, but don't worry about it for a second. Wouldn't think of it. So happy to be of help. I'm glad you are feeling better." No, Elisha's refusal had nothing to do with showing himself to be a generous man. This is not a "good guy" story. Rather, his refusal has everything to do with a jealous and holy God—a God who will not share responsibility or glory for the work of salvation. That is why Elisha began with an oath used often in this part of the Old Testament: *As surely as the* LORD *lives, whom I serve*, I will not accept a thing" (2 Kings 5:16).

Elisha was servant of the Most High God, and he knew he was standing on holy ground.

The reason he used the oath was both to remind himself of whose business he was in and to testify of that truth to others. It is not a bad idea in all our communications with others to think these words, or even say them out loud if needed, before giving responses. It purifies the conversation and keeps us on the right track. We get ourselves into lots of trouble when we forget whose business we are in, and whom we have to answer to. If Elisha needed to remind himself, we do, too.

Further, Elisha knew that this was not his miracle. For him to accept a gift from Naaman would make him a liar. Elisha would be saying to Naaman that he should be credited for the healing, when he knew that it was God's work alone. It would be as if I accepted payment for something that you had done. Elisha was no liar.

The great prophet would not take credit for God's miracle. Naaman seems to have concluded the same: when he exclaimed, "Now I know that there is no God in all the world except in Israel," he was testifying to his understanding that Israel's God was the One who had healed him, not Elisha the prophet.

We Christians have a hard time with this. No matter how long we have been believers, we want the credit. We want people to *ooh* and *ahh* over the work we have done; we want to be recognized; we want to reap a good reputation from the work that God himself has done in us. This is a more powerful temptation than the money because most of us would be thrilled to have accolades even without remuneration. This is part of our human condition, and it certainly was a temptation to Elisha.

I must make reference again to my father, a rural pastor in Iowa. On more than one occasion, an unbeliever offered him a gift. My father would thank the would-be donor but turn it down expressly because he did not want to give the impression that the gospel could be purchased. One could not gain favor with God by making donations to my dad or his church. He certainly did not turn away donors because the local church coffers were full—even my parents' whopping $200-per-month salary (out of which they supported eight kids of their own, as well as a couple of boarding students) was often paid late. It was tempting for Dad to take anything that was offered. But the free gift of salvation cannot be compromised.

There was another reason that Elisha refused a gift from Naaman. A little slave girl, still up in Damascus, laboring for her mistress, still a slave, was working for nothing. She was the one who had initiated this chain of events. She was the reason that Naaman was now standing in Elisha's front lawn, healed in body and spirit. She wasn't getting paid, and it was never in her mind that she would be. That was not her motive. She desired nothing more than that this very moment would come to pass, that Naaman would "see the prophet in Samaria," and that "he would heal him of his leprosy." For Elisha to accept a gift from Naaman at this point would be a desecration of her pure testimony to the grace of God for her master. The great prophet was not about to commit such a travesty.

THE PROPHET'S TEMPTATION

As all believers do at times in their lives, Elisha was facing strong temptation. But he knew that this was a trap, and he was wary. That is why his answer was simple, to the point, and immediate.

Shadrach, Meshach, and Abednego faced the blazing furnace if they did not bow down to King Nebuchadnezzar. They, too, answered immediately: "King Nebuchadnezzar, we do not need to defend ourselves before you in this matter" (Dan. 3:16). These young Jewish men and Elisha answered promptly because they knew that if they leisurely considered their answers, if they allowed themselves to roll the matter over in their minds, if they balanced and weighed all the pros and cons, they could easily go the wrong way. All of them were instinctively aware of the weakness of the flesh and the power of the Spirit, so they had nailed down their answers beforehand. But *someone* tries to get all of us to take a little time to consider all the angles at pivotal moments like this.

Do you smell a rat? Satan is intruding. Immediately after Naaman made his confession "there is no God in all the world except in Israel"—a conviction placed in his mind and heart by the God he professed—the devil entered the conversation. When Naaman offered money, Satan was using him to tempt Elisha. That is not to say that Naaman was satanic, but it is to say that Satan's influence was present. Elisha's refusal to accept anything may seem a small thing, but Satan knew very well that he would score a momentous victory if he could get Elisha to take the money.

This is much like Peter's great confession, followed by an explicitly satanic statement that tempted Jesus. Jesus asked his disciples, "Who do you say I am?," and Peter answered, "You are the Messiah, the Son of the living God." Jesus complimented Peter on his response, telling him that "this was not revealed to you by flesh and blood, but by my Father in heaven." But then Satan entered that conversation as well. When Jesus followed this by foretelling his death, Peter rebuked him by saying, "Never, Lord! This shall never happen to you!"

Jesus turned to Peter with stinging words: "Get behind me, Satan! You are a stumbling block to me; you do not have in mind the concerns of God, but merely human concerns" (Matt. 16:13–23). Both Naaman and Peter had good motives. But both Jesus and Elisha could see beyond what Naaman and Peter saw, recognizing what was happening cosmically. Jesus and Elisha were each being given an offer by the devil himself, each knew well that he was being tempted, and each gave a clear, unequivocal answer: "No." They could not and would not yield to the Prince of Darkness. They could not consider it for a second.

Why was this a watershed moment? Because in his refusal to take the money, Elisha was testifying to Naaman and to all of us through Scripture that the gospel of Jesus Christ is absolutely free. It is not for sale. You cannot pay for it even if you want to. "Come, all you who are thirsty, come to the waters; and you who have no money, come, buy and eat! Come, buy wine and milk without money and without cost" (Isa. 55:1). It is imperative that it be free of charge. If we were permitted to pay even a little bit, salvation would depend on us. That would be no salvation at all. When Elisha refused payment, he preached in a powerful and convincing way the free offer of the gospel.

GOD WILL PROVIDE

Furthermore, Elisha didn't need the money because God didn't need it. Before Naaman, he stood as God's spokesman. Elisha stood in God's place, and whatever applied to God applied to him. " 'The silver is mine and the gold is mine,' declares the Lord Almighty" (Hag. 2:8). And the Bible also says:

I have no need of a bull from your stall
    or of goats from your pens,
for every animal of the forest is mine,
    and the cattle on a thousand hills.
I know every bird in the mountains,
    and the insects in the fields are mine.
If I were hungry I would not tell you,
    for the world is mine, and all that is in it. (Ps. 50:9–12)

God doesn't need the money, and therefore we, as laborers in his vineyard, don't need the money either. This was a particular truth that Naaman needed to understand, as does every other child of God. As he had prepared for the trip to Israel, he never doubted that he would need to pay for what he obtained. Considering all the money he brought along, he thought he'd have to pay a whole lot. But Elisha preached the gospel of grace, and Naaman had to understand that it cannot be bought. Elisha took Naaman off the gold standard. From now on, Naaman, like all other believers, would have a set of values utterly foreign, unknown, and seemingly ridiculous to the mind-set of this world.

But Naaman kept after Elisha, urging him to accept a gift. Elisha refused again (2 Kings 5:16). Then Naaman could see that he was getting nowhere, so he stopped urging him.

So the payment-for-services matter was closed, at least as far as Elisha and Naaman were concerned. Sadly, however, this issue was not settled as far as the devil was concerned. We will take a look at that in the next chapter. At this time, however, Naaman accepted Elisha's answer as final.

NAAMAN'S FIRST REQUEST: A LOAD OF DIRT

Now this newborn child of the covenant had another request: "If you will not," said Naaman, "please let me, your servant, be given as much earth as a pair of mules can carry, for your servant will never again make burnt offerings and sacrifices to any other god but the LORD" (2 Kings 5:17). Isn't it amazing how the Lord works in new believers? Naaman had already memorized the first and second commandments, without studying them! "You shall have no other gods before me." "You shall not make for yourself an image in the form of anything in heaven above or on the earth beneath or in the waters below. You shall not bow down to them or worship them" (Ex. 20:3–5a). Naaman's instincts had undergone a sea change. A day or so before, he had thought nothing at all of bowing down to other gods. Now he found himself in a radically different universe. Already the Holy Spirit had put in him the keen awareness that there was only one true God, and Naaman already understood that the true God will not share his glory with any other.

NAAMAN WILL WORSHIP GOD

It is striking that Naaman, so soon after his miraculous healing, speaks of worship. It doesn't appear that anyone told him to respond in worship, yet he did. That is because worship is the natural instinct of a believer who recognizes the fact that he, a sinful creature, has been touched by the finger of God. So it was with Abraham's servant, who prayed in great detail for signs that he felt he needed to pick out the right girl for Isaac. Before he finished praying, the answers came in the same fine detail, matching the order in which they were prayed, faster than bullets from a machine gun. Amazed at this volley of right-on-target answers to his prayer, Abraham's servant was overwhelmed by the presence of God. "Then," Scripture tells us, "the man bowed down and worshiped the LORD" (Gen. 24:26).

This is the kind of worship that comes upon a believer without warning. There is no prelude to get you in the proper mood for the worship service. It comes the moment we have just tasted personally of his power, love, and personal attention, and we can do nothing but bow and worship. It is our new nature at work in us. All believers experience it at one time or another in their walk with the Lord.

Naaman now knew the heart of true worship, and he wanted to plan for the future. About to return to his homeland, he wanted to take some of Israel's real estate with him. When he had thrown a tantrum in the front yard of Elisha's house, before he was healed, he claimed a preference for the clear waters of Aram's rivers rather than the dirty Jordan.

But now he must have some of that dirt. So he asked Elisha for a load of earth—as much as a pair of mules could carry—to take back to Aram to build an altar so that he could worship the one true God. He knew that his worship could be offered only to the God of Israel: "your servant will never again make burnt offerings and sacrifices to any other god but the LORD" (2 Kings 5:17).

Why Naaman believed he needed to build an altar out of Israel's soil isn't explained here, but it is obviously intended to assist him in the worship of Jehovah God. Naaman indicates that he had previously offered "burnt offerings and sacrifices" to other gods, and he—again instinctively—believed that he should build a new altar.

We can understand his conscience in this. He did not want to desecrate the name of Jehovah God by offering burnt offerings on existing altars used for gods that he now knew to be false gods. Of course, it wasn't essential that such an altar be built out of Israel's soil. But it would serve as a continual reminder to Naaman and his attendants, when life got back to normal in Damascus, that this momentous healing had come from the God of Israel. An imported altar would proclaim not that dirt or water from Israel could heal and save, but what Jesus would later proclaim, that "salvation is from the Jews" (John 4:22). It would be a visible reminder to the Arameans that there was a prophet in Israel—that *there is no God in all the world except in Israel*.

NAAMAN'S SECOND REQUEST: SPECIAL PERMISSION

Then Naaman asked Elisha for something else. It really wasn't a request directed to Elisha, but to the Lord himself: "But may the LORD forgive your servant for this one thing: When my master enters the temple of Rimmon to bow down and he is leaning on my arm and I have to bow there also—when I bow down in the temple of Rimmon, may the LORD forgive your servant for this" (2 Kings 5:18). At first blush, this might sound outlandish. Some have even questioned the credibility of Naaman's earlier profession of faith. After all, wouldn't attendance and bowing down in an idol's temple be clearly prohibited? Naaman sensed that it might be, and that is why he asked forgiveness beforehand.

But I think criticism of Naaman for asking this favor is unwarranted. Some have said that in doing this he forfeited whatever blessings he would otherwise have received. He had been healed, but that was the extent of it. But I think it is remarkable that, at this early stage of life as a child of God, Naaman would ask the Lord to "forgive" him for assisting his master in the king's temple ritual.

Naaman was a military officer who had been trained to envision what a battlefield was going to look like "down the road" because he had to know what dangers might lie ahead. This is what he was doing here. He was envisioning life back in Damascus after he returned, thinking it through as he spoke: "I will never worship any god again other than the God of Israel. That would be sin. When I assist the king when he goes into Rimmon's temple for worship, I will not be worshiping another god. May the

LORD forgive me the appearance of doing so." And Naaman makes it clear that *he* would not be bowing down. It was the king who would be doing so, and Naaman would merely be supporting Ben-Hadad's body. Naaman shows in this request that he has at least an inkling of what true worship is, that it is in spirit and in truth. Elisha graciously adjures Naaman: "Go in peace" (2 Kings 5:19).

To conclude that Naaman's request showed a lack of faith would be inconsistent with Elisha's response. Elisha was giving Naaman a blessing when he adjured him to "Go in *peace*." The Hebrew word here is *shalom*. This was not merely a "good-bye," but a prophet's benediction upon Naaman and his life. Naaman was a believer, and believers have "the peace of God, which transcends all understanding" (Phil. 4:7).

This peace was God's word, through Elisha, to Naaman. It was not merely an accommodation of Naaman's circumstances as he prepared to face his official duties when he arrived back in Damascus because God does not make deals with idols or those who worship idols. This *shalom* was the Lord's unmitigated and unconditional blessing upon Naaman. Therefore, if Naaman is to be criticized here, shouldn't Elisha be criticized more? It is inconceivable that Elisha would confuse Naaman (and all of us) with a pronouncement of "peace" in response to a misguided request, if such an approbation would lead the new convert into sin.

NAAMAN'S TESTIMONY IN THE TEMPLE OF RIMMON

Elisha could also have said: "Go and *witness*." Do you remember the story in 1 Kings 18, where Elijah challenged the prophets of Baal? The prophets of Baal spent the day shouting out pleas to their god most of the day, to come down and burn up the sacrifice they had laid on their altar, but the god Baal, being miracle-challenged, didn't respond. Baal's prophets worked themselves into a frenzy, slashed their bodies, and screamed for an answer. Nothing. The sky was like bronze.

Then Elijah prepared his sacrifice on a different altar, flooded the altar several times with a well-known flame retardant (water), and simply prayed once to the Lord. The fire of God instantly descended, incinerating the sacrifice, the altar, the water, and whatever else was in the immediate vicinity. It was one of those times when God showed himself to be God by miraculous contrast to a false god. The same thing happened when Moses appeared before Pharaoh at the time of the plagues—the Egyptian enchanters could duplicate some of those miracles but failed at others (see Ex. 8:18).

It is the same here. The text is specific about what went on in the temple of Rimmon, the false god: "When my master enters the temple of Rimmon to bow down *and he is leaning on my arm*." Naaman and the king evidently did this regularly. Before Naaman's trip, the king would have been leaning on Naaman's sick, infected, contagious arm—if he had risked doing so. But now that arm would be healthy, like that of a young boy.

What would Ben-Hadad be thinking at such a moment? He must have already known that healing was not Rimmon's strong suit. Blocks of wood and stone find it difficult to perform healings; it's not their "thing." He also knew that Naaman had gone to Israel, on his orders, and that he had come back healed. Naaman would now be noising it about that there was no god in all the earth but Israel's God. From now on, every time the king bowed down to Rimmon, accompanied by Naaman, the stark contrast between the god of Aram and the God who could heal would be plain as day—and embarrassing to those who worshiped Rimmon. Naaman's accompaniment of the king to this ridiculous worship service was now to become a perpetual testimony.

No doubt Elisha had a gleam in his eye when he told Naaman to "go in peace." He knew that Israel's God was going to use Naaman to invade the temple of Rimmon, to shame false worship, to shine light into a dark place. The Lord can enter any room he wishes to enter, and he doesn't need permission.

RECONCILIATION ACCOMPLISHED

Note, too, that Elisha's benediction, "Go in peace," demonstrates not only that reconciliation between Naaman and God had been accomplished, but that reconciliation had been made between the "prophet in Samaria" and an enemy! This is what occurs when we are reconciled to God, when we are "brought near by the blood of Christ" (Eph. 2:13). And when we get near to God, of course we find ourselves near to those who are near to God.

It is remarkable that the prophet could dismiss an enemy in peace. There had to be great joy in both Elisha's and Naaman's hearts as they realized that the Lord had brought reconciliation between them. They stood as friends before the Lord.

NAAMAN'S JOYFUL HEART

So Naaman departed, heading back to Damascus. He was a different man now than he had been when he threw his tantrum and turned to go back after first talking to Elisha. How must he have felt? What kinds of things were going through his head as he settled in for this trip of more than a hundred miles? His brain was full as he recalled the incredible happenings of the past few days. He was thinking about all the events that had led up to his healing: the little servant girl, King Ben-Hadad's surprising support for this venture, the little fit he threw at Elisha's, his attendants insisting that he cool off and go through with Elisha's orders, his dipping seven times in the Jordan River, and his amazement when he came up out of the water—completely healed.

There were also greater matters to ponder. He understood now that there was only one God, the God of Israel. From his experience, Naaman knew that this God was personal, because he had dealt so intimately and personally with him. Naaman had been touched by the finger of God. Naaman knew that he had experienced a personal encounter with the God of the whole universe.

He had to be thinking, too, about all that gold, silver, and clothing weighing down the cart creaking along behind him. It had been of no use. It had to be taken back. It might have been the first time in his life that someone had refused an offer of money for services rendered. To say the least, it was unusual. He had received the greatest gift of his life—an unheard-of instant cure from leprosy—and Elisha wouldn't take a dime for it.

He looked down at his arms and legs: still perfectly healthy. "What have I done to merit this unfathomable favor?" he asked himself. He scratched his head, trying to figure it out. It didn't compute. That is, it didn't compute to the former Naaman, but he was now beginning to learn something of the amazing grace of Jehovah God.

Something else, too. Had he received special favor because he was a great general? But he had led troops *against* Israel. The Jews down there knew that he was their enemy. Yet for some reason far beyond his understanding he had been singled out to receive this great blessing, and from a *Jew*. Why? How? Could he have done something to deserve this singular act of kindness? No, he thought, I've done the opposite—I have warred against Israel, and right now I still have a little Jewish girl in captivity serving me as a slave. No, his reputation as a great military man couldn't be the reason he had been healed.

At this point, I'm sure that Naaman reached a conclusion, even though it seemed like something out of this world:

Israel's God loves me, even though I am his enemy! He had been reconciled to the only true God. He didn't have access to the book of Romans. He did not yet know in specific that this reconciliation would be brought about through the death and resurrection of God's Son (Rom. 5:10). But he knew that somehow he had been reconciled to God, and that in a personal, intimate way, God had become his friend. He couldn't grasp it all, but he knew it must be so.

He could hardly wait to share the good news, and in his mind he was already picturing what that would be like. For starters, he would tell his wife, his little slave girl, and the king. This would be Naaman's ultimate "show and tell" day—greater than any of the times he had returned to Damascus to report some military victory. Show them your arms, legs, face, scalp—all healed! Let them see how your flesh has been changed so that it looks like you were ten years old! Tell them what happened from start to finish, although you really don't know *how* it happened. Tell them about going back to Elisha's house, how you offered your gold, silver, and clothing to Elisha, and how the prophet turned you down flat.

Tell them that there is only one true God in all the earth—that worshiping Rimmon or any other god is a profane waste of time. Assemble your officers and tell them that Israel's God is not just a god of the mountains, or of the plains, or even of Israel alone, but that "now I know that there is no God *in all the world* except in Israel." Tell them that this God has befriended you, that he is a personal God, that he is the one who touched you personally and healed you. Tell them that you cannot for the life of you figure out why God chose you to be healed but that you will be forever grateful for his mercy.

Show them the load of Israel's soil that you brought back to Damascus and tell them that you need some help in building an altar to the Lord, and that you will no longer make any sacrifices or burnt offerings to any other gods. And tell them that you will need some of them to help you unload all the silver, gold, and clothing because every wonderful thing that happened to you was absolutely free. In fact, you were not allowed to pay anything even though you argued about it. Recite the words of Joseph Hart (1759):

> Come, ye needy, come, and welcome,
> God's free bounty glorify;
> True belief and true repentance,
> Every grace that brings you nigh.
> Without money, without money,
> Come to Jesus Christ and buy![2]

This was Naaman's buoyant, joyful testimony, building in his mind and heart, as he headed back home.

He and his royal troupe continued to wend their way up the road to Damascus, but presently they spotted someone approaching from the rear, and coming at a pretty good clip. As the pursuer closed the gap, Naaman ordered his convoy to stop. The whole company pulled over to the side of the road. As the man came closer, Naaman recognized him. It was Elisha's servant, Gehazi.

FOR FURTHER REFLECTION

1. What was the primary truth that Naaman learned from his healing? Is this important in God's work of salvation and reconciliation?
2. What is the primary cause of a person's coming to understand the sovereignty and supremacy of God?
3. What evidences are there in the text that the healing was God's miracle and not Elisha's?
4. Why is worship dominant in Naaman's thinking at this point? Where did this immediate desire to worship come from?
5. What testimony would Naaman carry back to Damascus, particularly to King Ben-Hadad? Do you think that Elisha had this in mind when the two parted?

CHAPTER EIGHT

GEHAZI AND NAAMAN

THE REST OF THE STORY

Paul Harvey was a celebrated media personality who died in 2009. During his career as a radio broadcaster, he created a popular show called *The Rest of the Story,* on which he would discuss a well- or not-so-well-known news item and tell his listeners some surprising additional facts about the event.

We have now studied the first segment of 2 Kings 5, contained in verses 1–19a, covering Naaman's healing and salvation. The last part of the chapter, verses 19b–27, is a record of "the rest of the story." The first part of the chapter is well known to Bible readers, but the part about Gehazi is often ignored. We tend to do this with stories and events recorded in the Bible if some of the story isn't as happy as the rest.

Take the story of Daniel in the lions' den, for example. We love to teach the first part about the brave Jewish captive Daniel—how he openly disobeyed King Darius's ordinance forbidding prayer to anyone but him. For his infraction, Daniel was punished by being thrown into a den of starving lions, where the Lord shut the lions' mouths, delivering Daniel from certain death. That's where we stop, though. We usually do not tell the part about the king's throwing the men who had accused Daniel into the same den—along with their wives and children—where their bones were crushed before their bodies hit the floor (Dan. 6:24).

We do the same with the story of David and Goliath, omitting the fact that after David killed the great giant with a sling and stone, he hacked, sliced, and chopped at Goliath's neck until the giant's head came off and then David carried the big, bloody head to Jerusalem as a trophy of war (1 Sam. 17:51). We tell the story of Noah and his family, saved in the ark, while we shy away from the fact that every other living person on the face of the earth—men, women and children—drowned in the great flood (Gen. 7).

We love to recount the parable of the prodigal son (Luke 15), who left his home but ultimately returned to be received back by his overjoyed father. But we hardly notice the "rest of the story"—the part about the older brother's arguing with his father and refusing to attend the welcome-home party for the penitent runaway. The parable ends with the older brother standing sullen and angry outside his home (vv. 25–32).

All these Bible stories and many more have this in common: a part that makes me smile and a part that makes me wince. Each contains a record of God's grace but also his judgment. We don't care for judgment. We prefer fairy tales instead, in which everyone lives happily ever after. But that is not history. It is not the real world, and it is not God's world. It is true that God's grace is greater than all our sin, and that in the end we will be taken into his glorious, joyous, sin-free heaven. Yet we must also learn of his hatred for sin, of the destruction that it causes us personally and in the world generally, and of the present judgment he metes out because of it. His mercy and judgment stride through history in tight formation.

We pick and choose to our own detriment. More significantly, we fail to teach the whole will of God (Acts 20:27) and to handle carefully the Word of truth (2 Tim. 2:15). God in Holy Scripture has given us exactly what we need for salvation and our lives. We will be wise if we take the bitter with the sweet, not merely because it is good to be realistic, but also because the harder part of the story is organically and inextricably related to the easier part; it is essential for an understanding of the whole. We deprive ourselves of the richness and depth of God's eternal truth when we ignore that which seems distasteful.

I once visited the Crystal Cathedral in California, at that time pastored by Robert Schuller, a self-professed positive thinker. When I visited the church's bookstore, I was intrigued when I saw a Bible designed to appeal to the positive thinkers among us. All the passages considered "positive" were highlighted in bright blue. The rest of the text was not highlighted. I had taught the book of Amos not long before and knew that it was filled with judgment from beginning to end. Just for fun, I turned to that book and saw no blue highlighting at all. I didn't look at 2 Kings 5, but my guess is that there was no pretty blue highlighting verses 19b–27 either. The record here of what Gehazi did is the hard part of this story, the part that we might not tell our children, and it makes us uncomfortable.

GEHAZI TAKES EXCEPTION WITH ELISHA

Gehazi had been there at Elisha's home when Naaman offered to make a gift. He heard Elisha's response to Naaman: "As surely as the LORD lives, whom I serve, I cannot accept a thing" (2 Kings 5:16). Gehazi heard the man of God, his master, say this, but he had a slightly different opinion. In fact, his opinion was the opposite. He believed that Elisha should have accepted the proffered contribution. In his mind, Elisha hadn't used good sense.

Gehazi rolled this over in his head after Elisha had bidden Namaan farewell. He had heard Elisha tell Naaman to "go in peace," but he didn't think peace should have been pronounced just yet—not until Naaman had stopped at the cash register. As he thought it over, Gehazi began to talk to himself about what Elisha had done. "My master," he muttered under his breath, "was too easy on Naaman, this Aramean, by not accepting from him what he brought" (2 Kings 5:20).

Gehazi thought that Elisha was getting too old for the job or had wax in his ears. In any event, Gehazi was having a hard time believing what he heard. After all, he was Elisha's servant and had firsthand knowledge of the household's financial condition. If there was anything they needed right now, it was money and a couple of sets of new clothes. That would reduce some of the anxiety around the place.

Indeed, Gehazi thought, not only had Elisha used bad judgment, but he had also unjustly passed up an opportunity to help the staff. After all, the staff and Elisha were all in this together. If Elisha wanted to be so generous, let him do it out of his own bank account. Elisha didn't have the right to speak for all of them.

Gehazi was upset with Elisha not just because there was a lot of money at stake, but because the whole thing wasn't fair. Not that the healing itself wasn't fair; he wouldn't go that far. Elisha had a right to do what he thought best in that area of the ministry. But Elisha wasn't the business manager. Considering what Naaman got from his visit to Samaria, to refuse his gift offering was at best inequitable.

"My master," Gehazi thought, "was too easy on Naaman, this Aramean" (2 Kings 5:20). It was bad enough that a man wasn't charged something for being healed, but doubly bad when the man was a foreigner, a heathen, an Aramean. An enemy of Israel! This wasn't the way to make your enemy sit up and take notice. Everyone up there in Damascus, when they heard that Elisha refused compensation, would think that these Israelites were a bunch of saps. No, Gehazi could not accept such foolishness. Elisha should have his head examined. It was a bad deal all the way around, and Gehazi was going to do something about it.

GEHAZI STRATEGIZES

Gehazi continued to talk to himself and began to make plans. "As surely as the LORD lives," he said under his breath, "I will run after him and get something from him." The phrase "as surely as the LORD lives" is used many times in the Old Testament as a strong affirmation, an oath. Elisha swore in the same manner when he refused Naaman's gift (2 Kings 5:16), although with the added phrase "whom I serve" (more literally translated "before whom I stand"), intensifying the oath by making particular reference to his servant relationship with God and to the fact that God was right on the premises, listening to and watching what his servant was saying and doing.

Elisha was acutely aware of these realities and acted accordingly. Gehazi was surely aware of them, too, but at least in this event he ignored the facts in order to satisfy his greed. Gehazi chose not to see himself standing before the living God. Here Gehazi was taking the Lord's name in vain in the most outrageous way imaginable: he was swearing in God's name to defy God himself.

How did Gehazi get here? In short, it was because he couldn't take Elisha's *no* for an answer. In the previous chapter of this book, we talked about Elisha's immediate response to Naaman's offer of money. Gehazi heard that response and didn't like it. Elisha didn't mull it over before he answered, but Gehazi did after that answer. Gehazi thought it over and came to the conclusion that Elisha had been too easy on Naaman; he thought it over some more and decided to go get the money; he thought it over even more and thought up a bunch of lies so that he could get the money. He did not see a blazing furnace, so he took his time, debated it, and did it. Once you start down that path, you're dead.

GEHAZI TAKES ACTION

The door of opportunity was closing fast because Naaman was already up the road a piece, and every minute was precious. Gehazi had to go after him. He knew he'd have to come up with a good story to sound halfway legitimate, but he could figure that out as he ran. He had likely faced this kind of situation before, when he had to make something up in order to get what he wanted. He could do it on the go. That part of it would be no problem.

When Naaman saw Gehazi running toward him, he got down out of his chariot. "Is everything all right?" a concerned Naaman called out as Gehazi approached. Gehazi was perspiring and gulping air as he slowed to a walk, stopping before Naaman. "Everything is all right," he answered. Then the tall tale: "My master sent me to say, 'Two young men from the company of the prophets have just come to me from the hill country of Ephraim. Please give them a talent of silver and two sets of clothing.'"

Gehazi could probably have gotten the same if he had just asked for it personally, given Naaman's sense of indebtedness. But Gehazi didn't want to leave that to chance. He had already used the Lord's name in vain when he talked to himself, so it could be considered a lesser included offense to use Elisha's name in a deceitful way. But this was a brazen lie, in at least three ways.

First, Gehazi lied in telling Naaman that the request for a talent of silver and two sets of clothing was Elisha's idea. No, it was Gehazi's idea, and Elisha had nothing to do with it. This was an abominable lie because it conveyed to Naaman that Elisha had changed his mind, that the oath "as surely as the LORD lives" in Elisha's refusal wasn't so very sure. So it submarined Elisha's word and reputation as a prophet of the living God.

The lie was also especially heinous because it defamed the God of Israel. If what Gehazi said was so, then God's word itself, spoken by the man of God, was pliable, iffy, and subject to change. Gehazi did not necessarily mean to undercut Elisha or defame the name of Jehovah, but he did so nevertheless, because he had his eye on something else. His singular focus was on the money, and that skewed everything. The God whom Naaman had just come to know is the same yesterday, today, and forever. He never changes, but Gehazi said that he did, and money made him say that.

Second, Gehazi fabricated the story about the two young men "from the company of the prophets" who were, he claimed, in need of financial assistance. This was a little bit clever, but not much. Gehazi told Naaman that these two young seminary students had "just come"—that is, in the short span of time since Naaman had left Elisha's house. So Gehazi injected an element of urgency into the request.

He had to, because he had to account in some way for the fact that Elisha had changed his mind so quickly. Gehazi had to cover all the bases. I will say this: such gilding of the lily comes naturally for those who lie. I know, because I've had considerable experience myself. Evidently I have had more experience than Gehazi had, because there wasn't a word of truth in what Gehazi said—not one. I've become more polished, finding it more convincing if the lie is lightly peppered with at least one word of truth. Lord, have mercy.

And of course, Gehazi never intended to share the money with anyone. He was going to keep it for himself.

NAAMAN COMPLIES WITH
GEHAZI'S REQUEST

Naaman was more than willing to comply with Gehazi's request. "'By all means, take two talents,' said Naaman.

He urged Gehazi to accept them, and then tied up the two talents of silver in two bags, with two sets of clothing. He gave them to two of his servants, and they carried them ahead of Gehazi" (2 Kings 5:23).

Gehazi had resurrected a mistaken idea in Naaman's mind. Gehazi told Naaman that Elisha had commissioned him to run this errand. Now Naaman believed that Elisha would accept payment. It may be that Naaman thought, at the time, that this was a minor detail. He was happy to have been asked. It would make him feel better, less indebted. But whatever Naaman's reaction was, Gehazi had misled him regarding a most solemn matter. Just as he had done with Elisha, Naaman "urged" Gehazi, this time to double his request for silver. "Take two talents! And two sets of clothing!" he said.

So of course Gehazi gobbled up all he could get, and then probably wished he had asked for more, particularly since the askings were being doubled. He took the money and the raiment. It worked out perfectly that Naaman would give him one talent for each student, together with one set of clothing for each. They ought to be able to get by for at least a semester on that.

This was not chump change. The talent is estimated to be about 75 pounds, so this was 150 pounds of silver—too heavy for the average man to lift, let alone carry. It was only 20 percent of Naaman's silver. Maybe Gehazi should have thought about taking all the gold—6,000 shekels, also estimated at 150 pounds. But he took what he took, and because it was too heavy for one man, Naaman lent two of his servants to Gehazi to help him with it.

Picture this pathetic scene. Naaman had halted his chariots, horses, carts, and attendants. They had to wait for the servants to complete their errand. They all stood there watching as Gehazi and the two servants lugged the treasure away, up a hill. When they got to the top of the hill, Gehazi dismissed them and said that he would take it the rest of the way. He figured that he had to, in order to sneak into town, stow the treasure in his house, and hide it away. He didn't want anyone in Elisha's camp to happen upon him accompanied by two of Naaman's servants. That might raise eyebrows.

NAAMAN'S ALTERED TESTIMONY

Consider the impact that Gehazi's flagrant, deceitful act had on Naaman's perception and testimony. He had to be confused. Elisha had been resolute, so why had he changed his mind? Was he being invited to pay something for Elisha's services after all?

Still, he could not wait to share the good news with everyone back in Damascus. He could still show them the skin that was perfectly clear, like that of a young boy. But now he would also have to tell them that although he got a good deal, it wasn't as good as he had first been led to believe. He had to pay something for it. He had to pay something to become acquainted with the God of the whole universe. Apparently Israel's god wasn't a whole lot different from Rimmon in this respect.

Naaman's message was altered. He now saw that Elisha owned a franchise on the grace of God. Elisha could charge for dispensing that grace. It was no longer free grace, not completely. Naaman could no longer sing this line of Joseph Hart's hymn: "Without money, without money, come to Jesus Christ and buy."[1] No, you might not have to bring very much, but you have to bring some. Israel's God had befriended Naaman, but his friendship cost something. And if the gospel costs even a nickel, it is no gospel at all, because it cannot be guaranteed (Rom. 4:16).

GEHAZI ATTACKED THE
HEART OF THE GOSPEL

This was a travesty, because Gehazi had attacked the soul of the gospel. It arose from Gehazi's belief that Elisha had been "too easy" on Naaman. That sounds familiar. This was exactly what the scribes and Pharisees constantly complained about when Jesus had dinner with tax collectors, prostitutes, and sinners of all kinds. It was how they condemned Jesus when he healed a man born blind, claiming that the man had been born in sin, and when he pardoned the woman caught in adultery. You are being too easy on them.

Luke 15 begins with a criticism of Jesus: "Now the tax collectors and sinners were all gathering around to hear Jesus. But the Pharisees and the teachers of the law muttered, 'This man welcomes sinners and eats with them'" (Luke 15:1–2). Jesus responds with three parables: the lost sheep, the lost coin, and the lost son. In the third, the parable of the prodigal son, Jesus returns their criticism (Luke 15:11–32).

A man had two sons, one of them who behaved himself and one who did not. A law partner of mine called such a recalcitrant son a "foul ball." The first did the chores faithfully, but the younger son acted the fool, wangling his inheritance out of his father and then leaving home. He got as far away from his family as he could, thinking that such independence and freedom would lead him to personal fulfillment and happiness. But after a time, he ran out of money and was not as happy or fulfilled as he had imagined.

He got what he wanted but did not want what he got. In fact, he became a beggar and found himself eating leftovers—not from the refrigerator, but from pigs. He began to think about how stupid he had been. He remembered his father's farm where he had once worked; he remembered the good meals they had every time they sat down at the table; he remembered that they always had lots of leftovers to put in the refrigerator. But he also knew that he had decided to turn his back on all of that, scuttling his inheritance and everything that went with it. He couldn't get it back now. That part of his life was over.

But he was in a predicament, and had no choice but to go back home. So, he thought, when I return it will have to be hat in hand. I'll tell my dad exactly how I feel—that I'm sorry that I did this foolish thing. Then I'll offer to go to work for him, this time as a hired servant. He didn't know if that would fly, but he had no other options. So the young man traveled home. As he neared home—but was still "afar off"—his father, sitting on the porch, saw him approaching. He gathered up his robe and ran to meet him. He ordered his servants to kill the fattened calf and threw a great welcome-home party for his foolish but repentant son. Jesus continues the story:

> Meanwhile, the older son was in the field. When he came near the house, he heard music and dancing. So he called one of the servants and asked him what was going on. "Your brother has come," he replied, "and your father has killed the fattened calf because he has him back safe and sound."
>
> The older brother became angry and refused to go in. So his father went out and pleaded with him. But he answered his father, "Look! All these years I've been slaving for you and never disobeyed your orders. Yet you never gave me even a young goat so I could celebrate with my friends. But when this son of yours who has squandered your property with prostitutes comes home, you kill the fattened calf for him!"
>
> "My son," the father said, "you are always with me, and everything I have is yours. But we had to celebrate and be glad, because this brother of yours was dead and is alive again; he was lost and is found." (Luke 15:25–32)

The older brother was so angry that he would not even come in the house to greet his brother. He had worked hard and faithfully for his father all his life. He could hear the music and dancing as he came near the home and couldn't believe it when he looked in the window and discovered what it was all about. To participate in a party like that for his lazy runaway brother was unthinkable and repugnant to him.

The late scholar and preacher Edmund Clowney often preached on this parable. He would say that you could hear the weary labor in the older brother's words: "All these years I've been slaving for you, and now you throw a party for someone who clearly doesn't deserve it. If anyone deserves a party, it's me. You've never done that for me. It just isn't fair. You are being too easy on this profligate."

This tax collector. This sinner. This prodigal brother. This Aramean. You are being too easy on them. Gehazi, the teachers of the law, the Pharisees, and the elder brother were all in the same boat. They did not see what the little slave girl, Elisha, Jesus, and the prodigal's father saw. They did not see a poor sinner in need of healing, cleansing, friendship, and welcome. They did not see the free and abundant grace of God. They did not see that "where sin increased, grace increased all the more" (Rom. 5:20). All of them, by their own sad choice, were thereby excluded from the joyful celebration of the saints of God.

That is exactly what Satan wants. What Gehazi exhibited in this incident is what Satan has always promoted: greed, love of money, self-centeredness, and destruction of gospel witness. Satan despises true reconciliation and knows that if he succeeds in these areas, he will isolate us from God and his people. Satan wants men and women to be just like him: standing outside and refusing to come in.

Gehazi, like the older son, had worked hard "all these years" for his master and hadn't gotten rich doing so. He had justified his actions by his own "fairness" standard, though his conscience must have bothered him significantly because he lied, sneaked into town, and hid the money in his house. Now he had to cook up another whopper to keep what he had done a secret.

FOR FURTHER REFLECTION

1. If you attended Sunday school as a child, do you remember hearing only portions of some Bible stories? Why do you think you were told only part of the story? Do you think this was wise?

2. What evidence do you see that indicates that Satan was involved in Gehazi's thinking and actions? What do you think Satan's motives and objectives were?

3. How is it that money often influences us to make bad choices and compromise our principles? Have you ever compromised because of money? If so, why do you think you took actions that you knew were unwise?

4. What effect did Gehazi's actions have on Naaman? What effect did they have on Naaman's understanding of what had occurred and on his testimony?

5. In what ways was Gehazi like the Pharisees? Why was Jesus so often outraged at what the Pharisees taught? How and why does a pharisaic attitude damage the work of reconciliation?

CHAPTER NINE

GEHAZI AND ELISHA

GEHAZI FACES THE MUSIC

Gehazi had to report to Elisha, at least if he wanted to keep his job. So after locking the bags of money and clothes in the cellar, he went in and stood before his master, reporting for duty. He was hoping Elisha would give him an errand to run or some other routine job, a clue that Elisha was blissfully unaware of his nefarious junket. He feared, though, that there was a remote chance that Elisha would ask him the very question that Elisha did ask: "Where have you been, Gehazi?" (2 Kings 5:25). This is a devastating question when you have been someplace you should not have been.

Gehazi's answer was another bald-faced lie, and a dumb one: "Your servant didn't go anywhere." This was beyond foolish. Gehazi had been around the prophet long enough to know that you couldn't keep a secret from him. If there was anyone in the world who should have known that this was plain stupid, it was Gehazi.

More, even if he hoped that this one would get by Elisha, he should have remembered what he and all believers know well—that God himself was present at the time and saw the whole episode. But we should not be shocked by Gehazi's irrationality, because sin is irrational at its root. I've always marveled at the Jews' response to Jesus after he raised Lazarus from the dead: They wanted to kill him! Because he could raise people from the dead? Does that sound like a plan? Luther's previously noted observation applies here as well: sin makes us "crazy."[1]

If it is stupid to lie to Elisha about where you have been, it is insane to try it with the Lord himself. But this wasn't the first or the last time such a lie has been attempted. After Adam and Eve ate the forbidden fruit in the garden of Eden, they hid from the Lord. The Lord came looking for them and called out, "Where are you?" Adam replied that he had tried to hide from him because he was naked. But of course, that wasn't quite it. The Lord had seen him naked from the beginning (Gen. 3:8–11). The real reason he tried to hide was that he had disobeyed the Lord, and was now afraid. When Cain murdered Abel, the Lord asked him where his brother was. Cain knew exactly where he had put the body, but he tried to lie his way out of it. "I don't know. Am I my brother's keeper?" (Gen. 4:9).

And in the first chapter of Job, the Lord puts the same question to Satan. Satan's answer was a lie because the truth was not in him: "from roaming throughout the earth, going back and forth on it" (Job 1:7). It was a lie because it was a half-truth. You know, I've been hanging out, sightseeing. But in fact he had been going back and forth in the earth, but "like a roaring lion looking for someone to devour" (1 Peter 5:8).

These lies did not work with the Lord, and Gehazi's lie was going nowhere with Elisha. Elisha wasn't fooled. "Was not my spirit with you when the man got down from his chariot to meet you?" Elisha knew what had happened not just in general, but in specific. By the power of the Holy Spirit, he had seen the event, every detail. Gehazi now knew he was fried tomatoes. He hadn't gotten away with a thing.

There is not another word from Gehazi recorded in this story because he had nothing left to say, and perhaps also because he realized that anything he might say couldn't be trusted anyway. I've been there, and I know exactly how Gehazi felt—condemned, humiliated, shamed, speechless, and naked as Adam. The lies were over. What an ass he had been.

ELISHA'S REBUKE

But Elisha wasn't through. He asked Gehazi, rhetorically, "Is this the time to take money or to accept clothes— or olive groves and vineyards, or flocks and herds, or male and female slaves?" (2 Kings 5:26). Gehazi, don't you realize that we are always standing before the living God? Look at what kind of day this is! Don't you see that it is a day of healing and joy, a day of salvation for a lost sinner? Don't you realize that a prodigal son has come home, that he was lost, but now is found?

Gehazi, have you been with me all these years and still do not understand that we are not in this for the money? That we do not own a franchise on the gospel? Do you not understand that this free grace of the God of Israel is not ours to sell? Why in the world would you take money or accept clothes from Naaman? Or anything at all? This is not a time for trading, but a day for worship because we have witnessed firsthand God's amazing grace!

Think again of Jesus' parable of the lost son. The elder brother's father pleaded with him to come into the house, because this was a day "to celebrate and be glad, because this brother of yours was dead and is alive again; he was lost and is found." But both the older brother and Gehazi were blind to the mercy, wonder, and glory of the day. Both of them, by their own choice, were left outside the house where the joyful welcome-home party was going on.

SLAVE-GIRL TRAVESTY

When Gehazi heard the last item in Elisha's rhetorical question, it was a knife in his heart. "Is this a day to trade female slaves?" Elisha's list of items is a circling hawk, homing in on its prey. It is no accident that Elisha emphasized the trading of female slaves by listing it last because this was exactly what Gehazi had done.

Gehazi surely knew about the little slave girl and her loving enthusiasm for her master, about her pure testimony to Naaman and simple assurance that the prophet in Israel would heal him of his leprosy. She expected nothing; 150 pounds of silver and two new dresses did not cross her mind. Her only desire was that her master would come home healed.

But Gehazi was a carpetbagger. He saw this event as an opportunity to make some money for himself and so traded on her testimony to make that happen. Further, he wasn't even directly involved in Naaman's healing or any of the events that led to it. While this little girl remained in bondage far away in a foreign land, separated from her parents, he was trimming Naaman for a small fortune because of what she had done. Gehazi had betrayed a poor child. No, Elisha remonstrated, this is not the time to be cashing in on captive maidservants.

THE PROPHET IMPOSES DISCIPLINE

Gehazi could do nothing but look down at his shoes. But Elisha continued, delivering this devastating consequence: "Naaman's leprosy will cling to you and to your descendants forever" (2 Kings 5:27). This is not the first time that God had punished a believer in this way. Miriam was sister to Moses, and together with Aaron rebelled against Moses (Num. 12). The Lord struck her with leprosy because she had not honored God's chosen leader. Aaron and Moses begged for mercy. Aaron cried out to Moses: "Please, my lord, I ask you not to hold against us the sin we have so foolishly committed. Do not let her be like a stillborn infant coming from its mother's womb with its flesh half eaten away" (Num. 12:11–12). So Moses cried out to the Lord: "Please,

God, heal her!" The Lord answered Moses' prayer and was gracious to Miriam; she was put outside the camp for seven days and then brought back in, healed of her leprosy.

Another instance involved Uzziah, who pleased the Lord for the better part of his reign as king of Judah. But when he assumed to himself the privileges of the priest, and was cautioned to stop, his pride led to anger, and the Lord struck him with leprosy, too. From that day on, "he lived in a separate house—leprous, and excluded from the temple of the LORD" (2 Chron. 26:21).

Now Gehazi had been punished with leprosy. Gehazi "went from Elisha's presence and his skin was leprous—it had become as white as snow" (2 Kings 5:27). What an awful judgment to inflict on the man. But it demonstrates how egregious it is to undermine the free grace of God and the message of the gospel.

Both Naaman and Gehazi were miraculously touched by the hand of the man of God. Naaman walked into his presence with leprosy and departed with skin like that of a child. Gehazi came into his presence healthy and walked out afflicted with the dread disease. As mentioned before, God's mercy and judgment are always present, working together, as his sovereign will is accomplished.

BEWARE JUDGMENTAL ATTITUDES

Having reviewed Gehazi's sin—his greed, deceit, theft, and more—we might be so inflamed with righteous judgment that we would say he got exactly what he deserved, maybe even got off easy. We may have the same mind-set that we often experience upon a reading of Romans 1, where Paul describes the world's progressive descent into sin, a mind-set that is bubbling over with righteous indignation at "them."

Paul quickly cures that attitude in Romans 2:1: "You, therefore, have no excuse, you who pass judgment on someone else, for at whatever point you judge another, you are condemning yourself, because you who pass judgment do the same things." Besides, judging others is not our domain. It is the Lord's province alone.

Gehazi's sin brought horrifying personal consequences, but his sin is not at all unfamiliar to us. How many times have I lied, colored the truth, or misled another because I wanted something right now that the lie would yield? When I do so, I am thinking, at least for that moment, that God doesn't see or hear—or perhaps I choose to ignore God's presence. I am just like Gehazi. I deserve a good whipping, too.

Elisha "transferred" Naaman's leprosy to Gehazi. This is not just poetic justice, though it is ironic. The awful malady that afflicted Naaman the Aramean now clung to Gehazi, a son of the covenant. Even aside from the pain and disfigurement that Gehazi would suffer, it also meant that for the rest of his life he could expect to be ostracized from normal social life. "For it is time for judgment to begin with God's household" (1 Peter 4:17). It is the greatest privilege imaginable to be chosen as a child of God, but it is no picnic. It is deadly serious business.

Gehazi was learning a hard lesson. There are many ways in which he had Naaman's clinging disease. Before he was born again, Naaman had trusted in his money. Gehazi's actions showed that he, too, trusted in money— even to the extent that he would conjure up a series of lies to get and keep it. Naaman, before the Jordan River, had insisted on doing things his way, and Gehazi had done the same. Naaman, because of his leprosy, was in dire need of the grace of the God of all the world. Gehazi now is in painfully obvious need of that same grace.

GOD'S GRACE FOR ALL

And God's free grace was abundantly available to both, because "where sin increased, grace increased all the more"

(Rom. 5:20). Indeed, the slave girl's exclamation stands as good news not just for the Naamans of the world, but for the Gehazis, too. It is more than an evangelistic utterance. The good news is for those outside and those inside the family of God. Those of us who have been through sin like Gehazi's will testify to just how essential, and how real, God's healing power is.

God disciplines his own, yet his mercy has no limits. It does appear that Elisha kept Gehazi on as his servant, because he is identified as such in 2 Kings 8. It is possible that he had been healed by that time because he had apparently not been fully quarantined. Whether healed in this life or not, as a child of God he always was, is, and would be under the sovereign mercies of his God. God never forsakes his own.

Naaman's perspective had radically changed after his meeting with Elisha. Gehazi's did, too, after his meeting with the prophet. When he got back home, things looked a whole lot different. He looked down at his skin and shuddered at the sight. As he examined his body, he glanced ruefully at those two bags of money and clothes. Now they looked hideous, and they made him sick to his stomach. Had it been worth it? He had Naaman's money, but going after it had required lie upon lie, and brought leprosy. Gehazi knew that his life would never be the same.

Gehazi not only was a child of the covenant, but had also been in an especially favored position. He had the same relationship to Elisha that Elisha had had with Elijah: he was the prophet's servant. When Elijah was taken up to heaven in a whirlwind, Elisha succeeded him, and with a double portion of his spirit. That was not to happen for Gehazi.

Elisha's transference of leprosy from Naaman to Gehazi was discipline. The congregation of which I am a member regularly disciplines, although to date not with leprosy! Thankfully, these occasions are rare, but when discipline does occur, the offending party confesses sin before the congregation and asks for forgiveness. The pastor admonishes the congregation to be mindful of their own weaknesses and, if they think they are presently standing, to take heed lest they fall (1 Cor. 10:12). This is no fun for any of us because when one member of the body suffers, the whole body suffers with it (1 Cor. 12:26).

But after this, the pastors and entire board of elders stand together with the member being disciplined to demonstrate their commitment to love, support, pray for, and encourage him or her. In these melancholy meetings, there is an unmistakable sense of family—family sorrow and also family love and care. There are always tears. The family of God comes together, demonstrating their absolute solidarity with the man or woman. We do this "because the Lord disciplines the one he loves, and he chastens everyone he accepts as a son" (Heb. 12:6). Biblical church discipline is a powerful bonding agent in the body of believers.

CHRISTIANS SIN AND
MUST BE DISCIPLINED

I have been on the receiving end of this experience—and I can testify to both the shame and sadness of the occasion and also the comfort. In about my thirtieth year of law practice, I misallocated client funds—a sin against the Lord, of course, and also cause for suspension of my license. I had practiced law for three decades and had been a Christian from childhood. I had been chosen for high office in the church. But there it was, right out there in the open before me and everyone else. Like Gehazi, all I could do was to look down.

But when forced to look in that direction, it is comforting to discover the *family* of God in a dimension probably not experienced before. I can tell you (and I hope that you never need to go through such a nightmare) that when you stand in front of the members of the body of Christ and confess sin, it is hard and liberating at the same time. You are ashamed, of course, but when surrounded by a loving family, the experience is not only something you can survive, but something very precious. The sin involved may have brought temporary alienation, but biblical discipline brings real reconciliation.

When Elisha made Gehazi leprous, he was in fact exercising this kind of church discipline. Gehazi was just like us in two ways: he was a sinner, and he was a member of the church. The church is family, the family of God, and that is a bond greater than any other relationship on earth. Sin is awful, but when a child of the covenant is publicly called on the carpet for his sin, he can take solace in the fact that his relationship to his family has not been altered. That relationship is absolute and forever. Because of his leprosy, Gehazi may have been quarantined from moving about freely in society, *but he was never quarantined from his family.*

WE NEED DISCIPLINE

No one likes discipline. We naturally do not want to admit to wrongdoing, and we certainly do not relish the idea that we might have to do so publicly. But as Christians, in our heart of hearts, after we give it full consideration, we actually do want to be disciplined because we understand that it is essential to our well-being. Would we want the Lord to allow us to continue down a destructive path that is displeasing to him? Would we want our hearts to become progressively colder and harder, insensitive to where our sin is taking us? Is that what we want to learn? Is that where we want to end up? Isn't it true that we have a deep desire to have God intervene? Do you now wish that your parents had always let you do as you wanted? David wrote, "Your rod and your staff, they *comfort* me" (Ps. 23:4).

Our prayer should be, "Lord, I desire your comfort more than anything. So I ask that you would apply your rod to me wherever, in your perfect judgment, it is needed." This may seem foolhardy, because when I so pray, I am really "asking for it." But at least it is a prayer that God will answer! And as he does, I will know without question that he is working in my life, that he will give me no more than I can bear, and that in the end I will have his comfort.

In chapter 2 of this book, we discussed God's use of trouble in a life to bring one to salvation. It is little different for straying believers. Trouble, from discomfort all the way to disaster, is typically the way in which God gets our attention. As a Christian, how many lessons have you learned, or how much have you grown, when everything is going well? It's possible, but rare.

It is not trite or unfeeling to say that though it was severe, Gehazi's leprosy was good for him: not as in "he got what was coming to him," but as in "your rod and your staff, they comfort me." If Gehazi was anything like I am, during the time he was planning his egregious act, carrying it out, and lying to cover it up, turmoil was building on the inside. And if he had exited his meeting with Elisha without the matter's having been brought to light, that turmoil would have grown more intense.

Every day following day would have been cat and mouse. Like a bank robber with a stash of cash, he'd have to be judicious in when, where, and how much he spent, so as not to raise suspicion needlessly. And the two sets of fine raiment: now, this was a problem, because there is no way known to man to use clothing like that apart from wearing it in public. Maybe those two items should stay in the basement. And we can imagine other difficulties if Gehazi were to keep this thing hidden, long-term. David testified in Psalm 32 about the pressure that builds before confession, and the relief that follows:

When I kept silent,
    my bones wasted away
    through my groaning all day long.

For day and night
    your hand was heavy on me;
my strength was sapped
    as in the heat of summer.

Then I acknowledged my sin to you
    and did not cover up my iniquity.
I said, "I will confess
    my transgressions to the LORD."
And you forgave
    the guilt of my sin. (Ps. 32:3–5)

When Gehazi left Elisha's presence, he had leprosy for sure, but a peace was also present because he no longer had to cover up. At least he could relax, and when he talked to his boss again, he could look him straight in the eye. A persistent effort to cover something up is laborious and takes a lot of energy. It also produces ulcers. But once the matter is aired and admitted, the turmoil comes to an end. You may have to live for the rest of your life on this earth with visible consequences of your sin, but there is peace because your conscience is clear. The burden is lifted.

GEHAZI HAD NOT TURNED OUT—YET

Forgive me if I get you bogged down in my own experiences. I've been like Gehazi so many times. Thus I have sympathy for him, and not just because he got caught. The flesh took over, and being in the flesh Gehazi was not able to say no. Should he have been able to resist? Yes, but not in the strength of the flesh, and Christians do sin.

When we confess our sin, ask God and those we have offended for pardon, and turn from the sin, we are consoled in knowing that neither the sin nor its consequences are the end of the story. We are not a prisoner of our sins, nor are we defined by them: "for sin shall no longer be your master, because you are not under the law, but under grace" (Rom. 6:14). We do not look at Gehazi as the sinner-leper and think, "Well, that's it. It's a shame, but that's how Gehazi turned out."

No, Gehazi hadn't turned out. Nor have we. The chastened sinner has a sure hope for change, growth, and God's rich blessing in his life. We will find out in heaven how everyone turned out. We sinners can take heart!

THE LORD WILL NOT GRIND US FOREVER

One of the primary reasons we have hope, even while the Lord is applying his rod of discipline, is his promise that he "is faithful; he will not let you be tempted beyond what you can bear" (1 Cor. 10:13). We feel that we are being ground to powder, that God has utterly forgotten our predicament, and that the grinding pain will never cease. Then we cry out, "How long, LORD? Will you be angry forever? How long will your jealousy burn like fire?" (Ps. 79:5), and the Lord's answer comes immediately: "For his anger lasts only a moment, but his favor lasts a lifetime" (Ps. 30:5). The Lord knows that we are but dust, and he will not "plow" or "thresh" us forever. Good poetry can convey truth powerfully, and on this subject the prophet Isaiah shows God's concern for us when being disciplined:

> Listen and hear my voice;
>   pay attention and hear what I say.
> When a farmer plows forplanting, does he plow
>   continually?
>   Does he keep on breaking up and working the soil?

When he has leveled the surface,
    does he not sow caraway and scatter cumin?
Does he not plant wheat in its place,
    barley in its plot
    and spelt in its field?
His God instructs him
    and teaches him the right way.

Caraway is not threshed with a sledge,
    nor is the wheel of a cart rolled over cumin;
caraway is beaten out with a rod,
    and cumin with a stick.
Grain must be ground to make bread;
    so one does not go on threshing it forever.
The wheels of a threshing cart may be rolled over it,
    but one does not use horses to grind grain.
All this also comes from the LORD Almighty,
    whose plan is wonderful,
    whose wisdom is magnificent. (Isa. 28:23–29)

Isn't it amazing that the Lord so *comforts* us while he *disciplines* us? In doing so, he demonstrates his intimate understanding of what we are going through. Isaiah's language speaks precisely to our need. We sink into depression and discouragement, believing for a time that God has switched on his threshing machine, thrown us into its grinding teeth, and turned away to attend to other more urgent matters. But he here assures us that his caring hands are on the controls. He is not destroying, but refining. His purpose is to strengthen us and make us into people useful for his kingdom purposes, finding our fulfillment there, and he will not fail in reaching his objectives. As we think about this, we will be comforted, even as we feel the heat of the furnace, and will recognize that what the Lord is doing is really what we need and actually desire.

This passage from Isaiah concludes by mentioning the *wisdom* of God as the ultimate result of discipline. A believer, while undergoing the trial, may not even know this is what he needs or what God's objective is. But when it is over, a Christian will look back on the experience and understand. The result is a deep, abiding joy that results both from the discipline itself and from the *experiential* knowledge that the Lord has been intimately engaged in the believer's life. In the end, as Isaiah testifies, we will realize that God's plan for his children who need discipline is wonderful—it is *magnificent*.

GOD DOES NOT GIVE UP ON US

Gehazi had a past, badly sullied, but he also had a future. This is one of the great verities of God's grace. God does not bring us to a breaking point merely to smash us into a thousand pieces and abandon us.

At times I've been so beset by my sin that I've wanted to not go on. Sometimes I have prayed that the Lord would just let me die. Why would I want to go on after these failings? Why would God want me to go on, to spend any more time and effort on such a hopeless case? For the Christian, this time is particularly dark. It is different from when a person first comes to salvation, because that experience seems a clean break from the past.

But the child of God who finds himself in sin is vulnerable to deeper sorrow because he should have known better. He already had the power of the Holy Spirit, but that didn't seem to make much difference. It is terrifying, because he doubts whether he is truly a believer. But it is at just such times that God will break through the swirling, murky blackness and remind us that we will have his blessing in the future. "For I know the plans I have for you," declares the LORD, "plans to prosper you and not to harm you, plans to give you hope and a future" (Jer. 29:11). So it was for this despondent leper, still and forever a child of God.

THE HEALING BALM OF THE CHURCH

And it is after discipline that the fellowship of believers, the church, appears as a fresh, healing balm to the defeated and discouraged believer. This is an aspect of the church that most of us will not fully appreciate unless we have had personal need of it. This is when we begin to see pastors, elders, deacons, members, and others in the body of Christ in a new way, appearing as street lamps at dusk, quietly blinking on, one after another, slowly growing brighter to light the way. Brothers and sisters help us to stand again, to walk again, and with prayer and regular encouragement to set our eyes on a new future. The church does not merely discipline us. It pastors us, encourages us, and reengages us to work shoulder to shoulder.

Nor was Elisha merely Gehazi's disciplinarian; he was his spiritual father and pastor. Elisha did no "high fives" when Gehazi walked out with leprosy, white as snow. He cared deeply for his servant and friend. He felt the pain of his discipline as profoundly as Gehazi did. This was a man whom Elisha had discipled. He had invested his own life in this servant. Gehazi had worked closely with his master, even participating in supernatural events, such as the miraculous birth of the Shunammite woman's son and then the boy's death and resurrection (2 Kings 4:8–36). He had been an experienced and trusted servant. Was that all gone now? Was he to have no future as a servant of God?

DON'T CLEAR OUT YOUR DESK

We might think that after Gehazi's grand larceny, Elisha would judge that he had no choice but to give him a pink slip. Certainly we would expect demotion and removal from the front line of ministry. And maybe that was so for a time.

But in 2 Kings 6, we see Elisha ministering to his servant, probably Gehazi, and involving him in the prophet's work once again. In that episode, Elisha through the Holy Spirit could discern the battle strategies of the king of Aram, and regularly informed the king of Israel. Elisha was the Old Testament CIA. The Aramean king's officers advised their boss that Elisha "tells the king of Israel the very words you speak in your bedroom" (2 Kings 6:12), and the king of Aram deemed this an unfair advantage.

The king sent a "vast army" to surround the city of Dothan, where Elisha was staying, in order to capture the magical scoundrel who was leaking military secrets to the king of Israel. The next morning Gehazi got up early and saw the horses and chariots surrounding Dothan. He was fearful and said to his master: "Oh no, my lord! What shall we do?"

Elisha prayed for his servant. "Open his eyes, LORD, so that he may see." The Lord did open his eyes, and Gehazi looked "and saw the hills full of horses and chariots of fire all around Elisha" (2 Kings 6:17). It was then that Elisha struck the Arameans with blindness and captured them.

Some commentators I have read concerning this event are critical of Elisha's servant because he did not have spiritual eyes to see. But it is not typical to see such heavenly realities, and it is not human error or sin that keeps us from seeing them. "The angel of the LORD encamps around those who fear him and he delivers them" (Ps. 34:7), but have any of us actually seen him? No, Elisha was not reprimanding his servant for not seeing, but rather introducing him to a supernatural vision that only a few are privileged to experience.

It was the same at the Mount of Transfiguration, where common disciples were being specially treated to an uncommon glimpse of the wonder and power of God (Matt. 17:1–8). Elisha was doing for Gehazi exactly what Jesus would do for Peter, James, and John. Gehazi's sin did not disqualify him from this remarkable experience.

Elisha was encouraging Gehazi, bringing him to a new level of spiritual maturity.

Later, in 2 Kings 8, Gehazi appears as an evangelist, a witness to the king of Israel, testifying as to all the great things Elisha had done. Then, "just as Gehazi was telling the king how Elisha had restored the dead to life, the woman whose son Elisha had brought back to life [the Shunammite woman mentioned in 2 Kings 4] came to appeal to the king for her house and land" (2 Kings 8:5). Gehazi and the king were obviously amazed at the timing of her visit. This, too, was a miracle. The king ordered that her land be returned to her.

The Lord was using Gehazi as an instrument of his grace, much as he had used Elijah and Elisha. Gehazi was privileged to witness to a king regarding the power of God evidenced in Elisha, and then to preside over a miracle. And in doing so, he also brought about justice for a homeless woman who had lost her property. The Shunammite woman knew Gehazi well and surely was grateful for his presence with the king that day. Gehazi, though on record as a sinner of the first order, was thus privileged to be a minister of the gospel.

Gehazi is a great encouragement to Christians. We do not wish sin on any of God's children, but it is wonderfully reassuring to know that men and women in the long history of the church— in both the Old Testament and the New—have committed great sin, have repented, have been disciplined, and have then received God's blessing on their lives. This is what Jesus came for; this news lies at the heart of redemptive reconciliation. Repentant, disciplined, and forgiven sinners may have unsightly scars, but like Gehazi's, they are battle scars that bespeak victory. God still uses us. There are no pink slips in the kingdom of heaven.

FOR FURTHER REFLECTION

1. Why do Christians sometimes lie? Why do they believe they can get away with it? Can you recall what was

going through your mind the last time you lied? Were you considering the fact that God knows everything?

2. What are some of the reasons that the Lord brings discipline in the life of a believer? What is his ultimate objective in doing so?

3. What do confession of sin and subsequent discipline have to do with the work of reconciliation? Have you ever seen this happen? Do you think that discipline had a positive or negative effect?

4. Have you seen a believer restored to the fellowship of believers after he or she has sinned? Would you say that the relationship between the church and that believer was worse, the same, or better afterward?

CHAPTER TEN

ELISHA ENDS THE RAIDS

ELISHA'S MIRACULOUS MILITARY-INTELLIGENCE CAPABILITY

We cannot leave Elisha without consideration of another encounter the prophet had with the Syrian military, mentioned briefly in the previous chapter with regard to Gehazi's role in it. The story of Naaman's healing has to do primarily with individuals—Naaman's reconciliation with God, with his slave girl, and with the great prophet. This additional incident is corporate, an encounter between the countries of Israel and Syria. This story is also related to Naaman's little slave girl, because it closes by noting that the Syrians finally abandoned the very kind of enemy actions that had brought about her enslavement.

Naaman's healing apparently did not forever end the ongoing conflict between the two kingdoms. Syria, under King Ben-Hadad, continued raids on the land of Israel. One of these was a military incursion recorded in the chapter following the record of Naaman's healing in 2 Kings 5. Naaman is not mentioned as a participant in 2 Kings 6. It could be that he had asked for early retirement because he now believed in the God of Israel and that created a conflict of interest for him. Naaman knew it would be futile for his country to wage war against that God, but more significantly, Israel's God was now the God he served.

The story begins with a problem faced by Syria's King Ben-Hadad, and it frustrated him no end. It was a problem having to do with Elisha. The story is recorded in 2 Kings 6:8–23. Israel and Syria were in perpetual conflict. The king of Syria would order his troops to take up a strategic position hidden from Israel and camp there, presumably so that he could ambush Israel's troops as they passed by. But the plan was not working.

Elisha did not have satellites, drones, or GPS, but whenever Syria camped, the prophet would send a messenger to the king of Israel and advise him of the exact location of the Syrian campsite, saying:

> "Beware of passing that place, because the Arameans are going down there." So the king of Israel checked on the place indicated by the man of God. Time and again Elisha warned the king, so that he was on his guard in such places. (2 Kings 6:9–10)

BEN-HADAD CAN'T FIGURE IT OUT

If this had happened just once, Ben-Hadad likely would have charged it off as a lucky break for Israel, but the problem was that it was happening "time and again." It could not be mere coincidence. So, as kings are wont to do, Ben-Hadad became enraged. Of course he tried to figure things out strictly from a human standpoint, and he concluded, logically, that there was a traitor in his army: "Tell me! Which of us is on the side of the king of Israel?" (2 Kings 6:11).

But one of Ben-Hadad's officers knew what was going on; how he found out, we do not know. He assured the king that no traitor resided among them, but that "Elisha, the prophet who is in Israel, tells the king of Israel the very words you speak in your bedroom" (2 Kings 6:12).

This presented a significant problem to Ben-Hadad—a problem considerably more difficult than nabbing a traitor among his own troops. How could Syria's counterintelligence division combat this kind of spying? Jam radio transmissions? Hack the Internet? He should have known that one cannot interfere with the Holy Spirit's communications. This brand of military intelligence was in a different realm, and Ben-Hadad had not yet developed sufficiently advanced technology to deal with an invisible tape-recorder located in his bedroom, operated by the Holy Spirit on behalf of his prophet Elisha.

Rewind to Gehazi, after he had secreted the money he took from Naaman. Gehazi, like the king of Syria, knew that Elisha had been given supernatural powers, but nevertheless had tried to get away with his evil deed by lying to the prophet. What was he thinking? What was King Ben-Hadad thinking here, when he then ordered his officer: "Go, find out where he is, so I can send men and capture him" (2 Kings 6:13)?

There are few words that describe King Ben-Hadad's order more adequately than *stupid*. The king's order was exactly like Pharaoh's orders repeated ten times in a row, refusing to let the Israelites go free. Each of Pharaoh's orders followed directly on the heels of Moses' display of miraculous power, demonstrating God's supernatural interest and intervention in the conflict. But when the going gets tough, natural man says, the tough get going. Nixon famously said this, too, as he faced possible impeachment for Watergate.

And that is what Ben-Hadad decided to do here. He foolishly attempted to conquer the supernatural with the natural. Of course, he did this because he assumed that Israel's God was like the gods of Damascus, like Rimmon, who possessed some imagined powers but who were local and could be manipulated.

THE MILITARY LOCATES ELISHA

So Ben-Hadad's spies secreted themselves into Israel, asked questions, and found out where Elisha was residing.

"He is in Dothan," they reported to the king. This was good news to Ben-Hadad, since the ancient city of Dothan, about twelve miles to the north of Samaria, was much smaller than the capital city, and would be easier to surround.

And that is what the Syrians did. The king sent horses and chariots and a "strong force" to Dothan, a force large enough to surround the city (2 Kings 6:14). And the Arameans did this at night!—as though this would keep the information from Elisha, who up until then had reported every campsite they had chosen.

GEHAZI'S EYES OPENED

Elisha's servant, though, did not have his master's understanding. He arose early the next morning and saw that the great Syrian army with horses and chariots had surrounded them. Desperation set in. "Oh no, my lord! What shall we do?" Elisha answered, "Don't be afraid. Those who are with us are more than those who are with them" (2 Kings 6:15–16).

Then, for the benefit of his terrified servant, Elisha prayed: "Open his eyes, LORD, so that he may see." The Lord immediately answered Elisha's prayer. Suddenly the servant's eyes were opened to a vastly different dimension of reality. The hills surrounding Dothan were filled with God's horses and "chariots of fire," in a protective ring all around Elisha (2 Kings 6:17). God's invincible forces had been there all along, hidden from human eye. Elisha, by the power of the Holy Spirit, saw them, and now his servant saw them as well. But the Syrians, who had surrounded Dothan by stealth, did not have any idea that the Lord's armies were there. They were still in the dark, and they were to remain in the dark for a spell.

Not having Elisha's eyesight, and therefore not being fully informed, the Syrian army began to advance into Dothan's city limits, fully confident that they could now capture their quarry. But the great prophet prayed to the Lord again: "Strike this army with blindness." Just as quickly as the Lord had answered Elisha's prayer to open the eyes of his servant, he now answered the prophet's prayer by blinding the eyes of the entire Syrian contingent surrounding Dothan.

Have you ever had to stop and ask for directions? It can be a little embarrassing if you have been telling your spouse and the rest of the family, for the entire trip, that you know the way well. It is beyond embarrassing when an army needs to ask for directions, especially when they have to ask the enemy. Whether the Arameans asked or not, we do not know, but they were now badly in need of directions.

Elisha volunteered by telling them: "This is not the road, and this is not the city. Follow me, and I will lead you to the man you are looking for" (2 Kings 6:19). This blind, dazed army not only were on the wrong road, but were surrounding the wrong city and were now being led by the very man they were looking for! They were way off base, or at least that's what Elisha led them to believe.

ELISHA SPARES THE SYRIANS' LIVES

So Elisha led this visually challenged army twelve miles south to Samaria, Israel's capital city. At some point during the trip, they must have been disarmed because they were unable to resist when they arrived. When they got there, Elisha prayed once more: "LORD, open the eyes of these men so they can see." Again the Lord answered Elisha's prayer, and the Syrians' eyes were immediately opened. To their surprise, and surely to their dismay, they now found themselves right in the center of downtown Samaria, surrounded by Israel's army and at Elisha's mercy.

The king of Israel could hardly wait for Elisha's permission to execute these men. "Shall I kill them, my father? Shall I kill them?" the king asked Elisha (2 Kings 6:21).

One is reminded of Jesus' encounter with his disciples in Samaria, recorded in Luke 9:

> As the time approached for him to be taken up to heaven, Jesus resolutely set out for Jerusalem. And he sent messengers on ahead, who went into a Samaritan village to get things ready for him; but the people there did not welcome him, because he was heading for Jerusalem. When the disciples James and John saw this, they asked, "Lord, do you want us to call fire down from heaven to destroy them?" But Jesus turned and rebuked them. Then he and his disciples went to another village. (Luke 9:51–56)

In the human desire for victory, for taking advantage of a situation for earthly dominance, for establishment of a kingdom on earth, neither Jesus nor Elisha cooperated. Both rebuked the ones who made what appeared to be a commonsense, earthly request. Elisha would not accede to the king's request. "Do not kill them," he answered. "Would you kill those you have captured with your own sword or bow?" (2 Kings 6:22).

THE PROPHET WINES AND
DINES ISRAEL'S ENEMIES

Now Elisha had another amazing surprise command in his arsenal—amazing to Israel's army, to Syria's army, and to us. Not only are you not to kill these enemies, the Syrians whom you have surrounded, but you are to give them something to eat! And as it turned out, it was not just bread and water. It was a "great feast." I imagine that at this point Israel's king must have thought this to be "counterintuitive," as in "this is crazy!" Shouldn't we kill them, now that they are in our hand? Allowing them to live, and then giving them a great feast, didn't make any more sense than Elisha's refusal to take money from Naaman. Gehazi said: "My master was too easy on Naaman, this Aramean, by not accepting from him what he brought" (2 Kings 5:20). And here, Elisha is letting an entire enemy military contingent go scot-free, not just one officer. And giving them a farewell dinner to boot! But Elisha was acting in accord with Proverbs 25:21–22:

> If your enemy is hungry, give him food to eat;
>   if he is thirsty, give him water to drink.
> In doing this, you will heap burning coals on his head,
>   and the LORD will reward you.

What a picture this is. It is just a glimpse of the great wedding feast that Jesus related in parable form in Matthew 22. Those who had been invited did not respond to the invitation. So the king who had invited them told his servants, " 'The wedding banquet is ready, but those I invited did not deserve to come. So go to the street corners and invite to the banquet anyone you find.' So the servants went out into the streets and gathered all the people they could find, the bad as well as the good, and the wedding hall was filled with guests" (Matt. 22:8–10).

Imagine what those Syrian soldiers were thinking as they sat down to eat. What in the world was going on? Like Naaman on his trip back to Damascus, they had to be wondering why they had been so delivered, and so honored. They would not be able to return to headquarters with Elisha in tow, as they had planned. But they would return with quite a story. It would be a story about the great prophet in Israel who first foiled their hostile mission, and then invited them to a great banquet. Like Naaman, they had done nothing to merit this kind of treatment. Nor does any person who comes face to face with Israel's God of grace.

The treatment that these Syrians received at the hand of Elisha did have a specific effect. At the beginning of the story of the healing of Naaman, it is recorded that Naaman's little slave girl had been taken captive by bands of Aramean raiders. After the soldiers who had enjoyed the banquet in Samaria had returned to their master, "the bands from Aram stopped raiding Israel's territory" (2 Kings 6:23). The actions that had forced the girl into slavery were now reversed as a matter of official policy, and it was all accomplished by God's free grace. Not a drop of blood had been spilled.

But we will discover, as we look at the New Testament, that God's similar grace to the Gentiles did not sit well with the Jews.

FOR FURTHER REFLECTION

1. Why did King Ben-Hadad think that he could trump Elisha's miraculous powers? What can you tell about his concept of Israel's God?
2. What truth did Elisha's servant come to appreciate when his eyes were opened? Have you had a similar experience, when your eyes were opened and you were overwhelmed by an awareness of the protective presence of God?
3. What reasons might Elisha have had for sparing the Syrians' lives? Where else in Scripture do you find examples of this?
4. What do you believe Elisha's major objective(s) might have been in this occurrence?

CHAPTER ELEVEN

JESUS AND NAAMAN

ACCOLADES FOR JESUS

The little slave girl's enthusiastic referral of her Syrian master to the prophet Elisha started some invisible but powerful wheels in motion. The story doesn't end at the conclusion of 2 Kings 5, nor with Gehazi, and not even with the closing of the Old Testament. Jesus himself almost lost his life the first year of his ministry because of her testimony.

Jesus was about thirty years old when he began his earthly ministry. The Gospel of Luke records his first public appearance in the area of Galilee. He healed the sick and cast out demons. He performed such miracles in Capernaum, he taught in the synagogues, "and everyone praised him" (Luke 4:15). His fame and popularity were on a fast rise, and the news about this amazing man, now deemed a prophet, spread quickly throughout the whole region.

Then he came to his own hometown, Nazareth. Initially the enthusiastic reception he had been receiving seemed as though it would continue unabated:

He went to Nazareth, where he had been brought up, and on the Sabbath day he went into the synagogue, as was his custom. He stood up to read, and the scroll of the prophet Isaiah was handed to him. Unrolling it, he found the place where it is written:

"The Spirit of the Lord is on me,
   because he has anointed me
   to proclaim good news to the poor.
He has sent me to proclaim freedom for the prisoners,
   and recovery of sight for the blind,
to set the oppressed free,
   to proclaim the year of the Lord's favor."

Then he rolled up the scroll, gave it back to the attendant and sat down. The eyes of everyone in the synagogue were fastened on him. He began by saying to them, "Today this scripture is fulfilled in your hearing." All spoke well of him and were amazed at the gracious words that came from his lips. (Luke 4:16–22a, quoting Isa. 61:1–2a)

This passage of Luke's Gospel is a favorite among Christians. Like the Jews of Nazareth, when we read these words of Jesus, we, too, are amazed at his gracious words. What a moment it must have been—to see him stand, read from Isaiah, roll up the scroll, sit down, and announce that he, right there in their presence, was the fulfillment of this ancient prophecy! It was surreal. They were firsthand witnesses to, even participants in, this pivot point in eternal events. It would seem that the place would break out in a spontaneous singing of the "Hallelujah Chorus."

THE JEWS TURN ON JESUS

But in chapter 8, we talked about the importance of telling the "rest of the story." There is a sad last half of this story, too, and it doesn't include the doxology. The Jews of Nazareth began to whisper. Their whispers grew into open resentment, their resentment to anger, and their anger into a murderous fury:

> "Isn't this Joseph's son?" they asked.
>
> Jesus said to them, "Surely you will quote this proverb to me: 'Physician, heal yourself!' And you will tell me, 'Do here in your hometown what we have heard that you did in Capernaum.' Truly I tell you," he continued, "no prophet is accepted in his hometown. I assure you that there were many widows in Israel in Elijah's time, when the sky was shut for three and a half years and there was a severe famine throughout the land. Yet Elijah was not sent to any of them, but to a widow in Zarephath in the region of Sidon. And there were many in Israel with leprosy in the time of Elisha the prophet, yet not one of them was cleansed—only Naaman the Syrian."
>
> All the people in the synagogue were furious when they heard this. They got up, drove him out of the town, and took him to the brow of the hill on which the town was built, in order to throw him off the cliff. But he walked right through the crowd and went on his way. (Luke 4:22b–30)

Considered in isolation, apart from the rest of Scripture, the cause of the Jews' fury is not evident. You might see why they would get irritated, even angry, when Jesus told them that he could heal in Capernaum and elsewhere but not in his hometown of Nazareth. But drive him out of town? Try to throw him off a cliff? Murder him? There was something deep and raw in their hearts that caused this vicious, bloodthirsty response. Whatever it was, Jesus had torn off the lid, freeing it to erupt volcanically. What was it? What led to it? There are many reasons, but they can be summarized by examining three major components.

THE JEWS

The tone of the conversation had taken a sharp turn from their amazement at the "gracious words that came from his lips" when some in the audience began to ask the question: "Isn't this Joseph's son?" Isn't he just a local boy, the carpenter's kid? He grew up with us. He is one of us. Now he is walking into our synagogue claiming that *he* is the fulfillment of Isaiah's prophecy? How does he get off doing that? He has come with no credentials, and he hasn't documented that he is anyone special. This hometown boy has to prove himself. Show us one of your miracles before we go any further.

Jesus knew their thoughts as they thought them. He said to them, "Surely you will quote this proverb to me: 'Physician, heal yourself!' And you will tell me, 'Do here in your hometown what we have heard that you did in Capernaum'" (Luke 4:23). They hadn't said it out loud, but that was what they were thinking. Jesus was showing them a miracle they weren't ready for—reading their minds—and it was unsettling to them. Of course, he spoke exactly what they were thinking, and they knew it.

Jesus had been raised in a poor home, and that is how they remembered him. They looked down on him because of that. None of them looked at him as anyone more than their equal. To them, he was the common of the common. And now, in their estimation, he was coming back to town claiming superior office and character, and serious resentment was building. When Matthew recorded the same event, he described it this way:

Coming to his hometown, he began teaching the people in their synagogue, and they were amazed. "Where did this man get this wisdom and these miraculous powers?" they asked. "Isn't this the carpenter's son? Isn't his mother's name Mary, and aren't his brothers James, Joseph, Simon and Judas?

Aren't all his sisters with us? Where then did this man get all these things?" And they took offense at him. (Matt. 13:54–57)

They may have been amazed, but they were contemptuous. Jesus knew that this growing contempt for him was in their hearts when he said, "Physician, heal yourself!" They demanded that if Jesus were going to heal the sick, he had a particular duty to heal those in his hometown first. Conventional wisdom is that charity begins at home. You owe it to us. Show whatever miraculous healing powers you claim right here in Nazareth, as we have heard you did in Capernaum. Let's see you do it! Perform for us! Prove yourself if you want to mollify our skepticism.

Though they were wrong in thinking these thoughts and having these attitudes, I believe we can understand because, confronted with the same, we would likely respond as they did today. It as though a young graduate from seminary were invited to preach at his childhood church. Imagine the reaction he would get from the congregation if he announced from the pulpit that he couldn't preach there because the congregation didn't believe; that unbelievers and foreigners were closer to the kingdom of heaven than they were; that he would go elsewhere where people would have receptive ears and hearts.

No, when the hometown boy comes back home, even if he has made a name for himself elsewhere, he must show gratitude and appreciation to the locals, graciously accepting their congratulations, responding deferentially as in, "No, no. I never could have done it without you! This is where I grew up. This is where I have my roots." People would get upset with him if he did otherwise, and he would not be invited back, at least not until he learned how to show proper respect. It wouldn't be surprising to see some of our own walk out, too.

THE JEWS' PROBLEM WITH NAAMAN

But it was when the Lord cited the Old Testament records of the widow in Zarephath and Naaman's healing that the synagogue congregants lost it. His meaning was more obvious to them than it might be to us. He was issuing a severe rebuke.

He was saying that he could not do for them what he had just done in Capernaum for the very reason that Elijah chose to provide food for a foreign Gentile woman in a great famine, and Elisha chose to heal a Syrian leper rather than one of the many lepers in Israel. (There were indeed lepers in Israel at that time; see 2 Kings 7:3 and following.)

The Jews of Nazareth, who studied the Scripture assiduously, knew these stories well. Jesus was declaring that these foreigners, these heathen, these pagan Gentiles whom they despised were in a more favored position in relation to entrance into the kingdom of heaven than they were. And he was saying this to his own friends, in his hometown—more remarkably, to his *devout* friends—the ones worshiping in the synagogue. They were the faithful churchgoers of the day, the pillars.

If they had not been devout, they wouldn't have been filling the pews. They believed the Old Testament, the Torah (at least the parts of it that met with their approval), and obviously they read, listened to, and studied it because that was what they handed up to Jesus to read when he was invited to speak. These folks had studied hard and had developed a superior religion. They thought their richly ornamented religion to be based on the Scripture of what we now call the Old Testament, upon the writings contained in the scroll that Jesus had just read from.

But what Jesus called to mind from the scroll—the stories of the widow of Zarephath and General Naaman—in this context was to them flagrant heresy. It was flatly contrary to the "faith" of these "people of faith," and struck a body blow to the fragile, formulaic religion that they had constructed for themselves, upon which they had placed their hope.

In this we see that they had splintered the Word of God. Instead of recognizing that God's love for the Gentiles is evident in the Old Testament (think Nineveh), they hated the idea. They refused to accept the good news for anyone outside the bloodline of Father Abraham. They were picking and choosing. What parts of Scripture they approved of were those that supported *their* theology, and thus their false religion supplanted the Word of God.

The good news has a sting to it when preached to those who love its gracious words but reject the rest. One might ask this question of the Jews: If you believe the Scriptures, the scroll that you just handed to Jesus, how could you even object to the fact that two of your own prophets, Elijah and Elisha, performed these amazing miracles? "Well," they would answer, "we believe the stories, but we don't like Jesus' application."

But the gospel is not for those who want it only on their terms. To such people it becomes a threat. In other words, what the little slave girl had said to Naaman's wife was really not good news at all to these Jews. Her message, delivered to an undeserving Gentile sinner, seriously undermined the security they had placed in their religion.

The Jews of Nazareth believed that they were the special people of God. They took this to be the primary message and theme of the Torah. They were special because they were children of Abraham by natural lineage. They were special because they were the caretakers of the Scriptures, the Word of God, and in fact they were in a favored position because they were the ones who were "entrusted with the very words of God" (Rom. 3:1–2). They thought themselves favored by God because they had invented sets of rules, rules they thought to be based on Moses' law. They had even made *extra* rules beyond Scripture ("they worship me in vain; their teachings are merely human rules" [Matt. 15:9]). They thought these codes of behavior to be of utmost importance, too—more important than Mosaic law. That is why they spent the Sabbath at the synagogue, studying them over and over again. They also surmised that they were fairly good at keeping these rules, at least better than anyone else. They were sure that nobody alive could be closer to God, to the kingdom of heaven, than they were.

THE JEWS' ATTITUDE OF SUPERIORITY

Certainly, by any human standard, the Jews did stand in a superior position to Naaman. Naaman had not descended from Abraham. He had no schooling in Moses' law. He knew nothing about Jewish religious rules. He did not study them or give them credence. He didn't worship the true God, the God of Abraham, or even give him any consideration, other than believing that God had limited power to assist Israel's military when they fought in the mountains. That was not his God. He worshiped only false gods. He was a Gentile—utterly heathen, utterly unworthy. And Naaman was particularly unworthy because he had waged war against the Jews; he was an avowed enemy of the chosen race.

These synagogue attendees would not have permitted Naaman into their kingdom. But Jesus would, and by his reference to Naaman, he certified that he had already done so centuries before. He was declaring to them that even heathen enemies of Israel and foreign women were closer to the kingdom of God than they were. His rebuke to the Jews in this episode is the recurrent criticism he leveled at the Pharisees throughout the New Testament: "Do you begrudge my generosity?" (Matt. 20:15 ESV). But Scripture says, "God has mercy on whom he wants to have mercy" (Rom. 9:18).

The line of demarcation that the Jews had drawn between saints and sinners was wrong, and always had been. Their religion looked so good to them, but it was a sham because it consisted of superficial judgments based on externals rather than the heart.

Do you recall the Pharisee in Luke 18 who was confident of his own righteousness but looked down on everyone else and with a loud voice thanked God that he had not been made like other men who were sinners? And then how the sinful tax collector who beat on his chest and cried, "God be merciful to me, a sinner," rather than the self-righteous Pharisee, went down to his house justified? And when Jesus healed the man born blind from birth, how the teachers of the law threw him out of the synagogue because to them he was a hopeless, dirty, congenital sinner while they were righteous (John 9)?

On another occasion, Jesus infuriated the Pharisees when he told them that tax collectors and prostitutes were nearer the kingdom than they were (Matt. 21:31–32). And in an event parallel to 2 Kings 5, while the Romans were oppressing the Jewish nation, Jesus healed the child of a Roman officer (Luke 7:1–10), once again upsetting the Pharisees' view that Jews were closer to the kingdom of God than Gentiles were. The Roman officer told Jesus that it was unnecessary for the Lord to come to his home to heal his servant, but just to " 'say the word, and my servant will be healed.' . . . When Jesus heard this, he was amazed at him, and turning to the crowd following him, he said, 'I tell you, I have not found such great faith even in Israel' " (Luke 7:7–9).

These are just a few examples of how the Lord's categories distancing eternal life from eternal death differed from the Jews' ideas. Jesus was turning their categories upside down and inside out, putting them in the latter group and Naaman in the first, thus infuriating them because his gospel had become a severe threat to what they were banking on.

THE LITTLE SLAVE GIRL DIFFERED
WITH THE JEWS

On the other hand, Naaman's slave girl had it right. In her humble, unschooled, guileless, loving heart, she knew something about the kingdom of God that the studied Jews of Nazareth had completely missed. Eight centuries before Jesus was born, the Holy Spirit had instilled in her a simple understanding that the kingdom was wide open to a man when he got to the point of realizing that he was "weak and wounded, sick and sore" and that "all the fitness he requires is to feel your need of him."[1]

She believed that if a sick and helpless man would only ask, just go, he would find healing from the prophet in Israel. You did not have to be in Abraham's lineage. It didn't take laborious study. It didn't take good works or tithing. It didn't require a star for perfect attendance at the synagogue. It didn't take circumcision. It didn't require a Jewish law degree. If that is what you think it takes, you are lost. What it does require is recognition of utter helplessness, a bent knee, and simple obedience to the command that all men everywhere must repent (Acts 17:30). No one can get it on any other basis.

And because Jesus, by referencing the healing of Naaman, blew the foundation of their rickety religion out from under them, they were threatened. *He* was the threat. They had to go after him.

This explains part of their reaction to what he said. But these factors alone do not tell the whole story because the Jews of Nazareth were not the only ones present at the scene of the crime.

SATAN'S INFLUENCE

We detected Satan at work earlier, tempting Elisha with Naaman's offer of money, and tempting Gehazi with the same. He got nowhere with Elisha but did with Gehazi. That "old serpent, the devil," reenters the picture here, and his fingerprints are all over the room.

When the Jews defied Jesus, demanding that "you do here in your hometown what we have heard that you did in Capernaum," they were throwing down the gaunt-let, just as Satan had done in the passage immediately preceding (Luke 4:1–13). "If you are the Son of God, tell this stone to become bread," the devil said, challenging Jesus to prove his supernatural status. Or throw yourself down from the highest point of the temple, and prove that God will protect you and save you from death. No, Jesus said, and "do not put the Lord your God to the test" (v. 12). Satan was testing him, but Jesus did not waver. And Satan, tempting Jesus unsuccessfully three times, still refused to give up, leaving him "until an opportune time" (v. 13).

Satan could hardly wait to strike again, and he judged Jesus' visit to Nazareth to be the opportune time. Now he would use a different tack, not direct confrontation but managing it from the periphery. He would use those who had had the most influence on Jesus in his formative years, through those whom the boy Jesus had loved, looked up to, and respected.

Following Satan's lead, these citizens of Nazareth were now also demanding that Jesus prove he was divine. Like Satan, they were demanding it on their own terms. And though, as we will see, Jesus summarily dispatched them, this must have been a powerful temptation to him as a man in the flesh.

We know this because it would have been a great temptation to any one of us, and "we have one who has been tempted in every way, just as we are—yet he did not sin" (Heb. 4:15). Think of returning to your own hometown or neighborhood, after some heroic or amazing accomplishment elsewhere. Your reputation preceded you. You were coming back home with a measure of fame. Would you not want to demonstrate what you were made of, what you could do, and who you now were? Wouldn't it be gratifying to demonstrate this to your boyhood friends, the ones with whom you had grown up? They would witness it firsthand, be amazed, and applaud.

In Jesus' case, they would post a sign on the highway just out of town, reading "WELCOME TO NAZARETH, HOME OF JESUS," honoring him as a famous and good citizen. We might dream of that and ask for little more in life. I'd find excuses to drive into town as many times as possible, just to feast my eyes on the sign.

Jesus saw the ploy instantly. He knew who was behind this. It was Satan who was speaking through these people. Jesus recognized Satan's voice and knew what he was up to. As tempting as it might have been to give in to the desire to be well liked and highly thought of in his community, as tempting as it might have been to do this for the sake of family name—and as *appropriate* as it would be in this case—that was not his mission. It would be devastating to his mission if he were to yield. He had not come to prove to men that he had the ability to perform miracles, nor had he come for applause. He had not come for himself, but for us. He had come not for the superficial, but for light, truth, and the issues of the heart.

The people became insane with anger when Jesus mentioned Naaman. But they were not just acting on their own. Satan was influencing them. He was *in* them. They were acting as Satan's family. "You belong to your father, the devil," Jesus said in John 8:44, "and you want to carry out your father's desires. He was a murderer from the beginning, not holding to the truth, for there is no truth in him." Satan's frustration in failing now a fourth time in tempting Jesus boiled over in the Jews of Nazareth. The devil was a murderer from the beginning, and now they followed his example. They sought the ultimate, to put Jesus to death.

Satan's efforts here were more than indications of a bad temper. He had specific objectives. The most obvious, of course, was that he was determined to kill Jesus, for he knew what Jesus had come to earth to do. This determination continued unabated up through the crucifixion. He was foolish in thinking that he could succeed in destroying his Creator, but he was insane, and would try nevertheless.

Second, he wanted to keep the Jews in ignorance, still trusting their false religion. Satan often works through religion to accomplish his objectives. As we look at the world today, it appears that he has had immense success in doing so, because false religion dominates everywhere. But the devil is foolish here, too, because of the absolute certainty of the advance and ultimate coming of the kingdom of God.

A third objective here, and most significant for purposes of our study, is that Satan doggedly tries to frustrate the spread of the gospel. The last thing he wants is for sinners to hear the good news. He did not want the Jews of Nazareth to hear the truth about their religion. He wanted to keep both the Jew and the Gentile in the dark. Satan is the dark one. He obscured the truth and light when he talked to Eve, and he has been attempting to darken the light of the gospel ever since.

THE HEALING OF NAAMAN:
A THREAT TO SATAN

And now there was something more threatening to the devil's objectives. The gospel was going global. Jesus was implicitly but clearly announcing that the gospel was for the Gentiles, too—for everyone in the world, no matter what kingdom, tribe, race, or nation. Satan wanted that to end right here, right now.

Satan believed that up until Jesus had come to earth, he (the devil) had been pretty successful in keeping the Gentile world in the dark. He knew that he would lose ground big time if news were to be spread that the gospel was for the Naamans of the world, too. There are a whole lot more Gentiles than Jews. Satan wanted the lines that the Jews had drawn to hold firm, because that way neither Jew nor

Gentile would hear or understand the gospel. He had to stop the future advance of the kingdom that Jesus had just announced. He calculated that the best way to accomplish that was to do away with the messenger.

The Jews of Nazareth who did this deed—driving Jesus out of town and attempting to throw him off the cliff—were absolutely responsible for what they did (or tried to do). But Satan was there, and his murderous insanity was evidenced in them. Satan works through his own children.

GOD'S JEALOUSY EVANGELISM

God was working out his sovereign purposes in this event. He was in control of everything that happened. When the Jews exploded and tried to kill Jesus, they were, of course, acting contrary to God's will, but they were not outside his control. And God's plan was in no way injured, altered, or frustrated. Rather, his kingdom was being advanced. This was not a setback. Just as in the life of Job, here, God would actually employ Satan for divine purposes, the advance of the kingdom of heaven.

We may not know all the reasons for the Jews' anger, but Scripture provides us with some. Certainly they were jealous. They did not see how rank pagans could become members of the chosen race. It didn't seem fair. Yet this is exactly what the slave girl knew, and what Jesus preached. It irritated the Jews no end, and their jealousy got the best of them. Gehazi himself evidenced this jealousy—he objected to the fact that Elisha had been too easy on "this Aramean," and that the pagan got away without having to pay.

But this jealousy and envy, in God's sovereign plan, is an engine of evangelism to the Jews. This was set out when God spoke through Moses:

They made me jealous by what is no god
    and angered me with their worthless idols.

> I will make them envious by those who are not
>   a people;
> I will make them angry by a nation that has no
>   understanding. (Deut. 32:21)

The little slave girl surely did not comprehend it, but her announcement of the good news to Naaman was going to result not only in the physical and spiritual healing of a Gentile, but in evangelism to the Jews. The Syrians, so far as the kingdom of God is concerned, were "not a people"; they were a "nation that has no understanding." But through the little girl, Naaman was healed and came to know the God of Israel, enjoying priority over the Israelites. We know about this priority because Jesus said that "there were many in Israel with leprosy in the time of Elisha the prophet, yet not one of them was cleansed—only Naaman the Syrian" (Luke 4:27).

But the gospel to the Gentiles is not the end of the story. The Jews are not without hope, but it is through the *healing* of the Gentile nations that they will be saved. Paul said:

> Again I ask: Did they stumble so as to fall beyond recovery? Not at all! Rather, because of their transgression, *salvation has come to the Gentiles to make Israel envious.* (Rom. 11:11)

A godly envy of the Gentiles will bring the Jews to Christ. The Jews' rejection of the gospel "brought reconciliation to the world" (Rom. 11:15), and the reconciliation of the Gentiles to God will bring about the salvation of the Jews. This is not the way we would have planned it, because to us it wouldn't work. But salvation belongs to the Lord, and it is his way:

> Just as you who were at one time disobedient to God have now received mercy as a result of their disobedience, so they too have now become disobedient

in order that they too may now receive mercy as a result of God's mercy to you. For God has bound everyone over to disobedience so that he may have mercy on them all. (Rom. 11:30–32)

God did not cause the Jews of Nazareth to sin, because he is not the author of sin. But he used and will use the Jews' jealous fury to bring about his will. His will is for his own glory and our good, for "in all things God works for the good of those who love him, who have been called according to his purpose" (Rom. 8:28). The events in Nazareth that day were no accident. They came about ultimately for his glory, for our good, and for his kingdom purposes.

JESUS SAW IT ALL

Jesus left Nazareth that day without any visible indication that he had accomplished anything to promote the reconciliation of the Jews to God, to the Gentiles, or to their Jewish brothers and sisters. In fact, to the human eye it looked as though that particular Sabbath day was a setback. When Jesus came into town, they had welcomed him. Before he left, they had tried to kill him. They had attempted to murder the very One, and the only One, who could accomplish the great ministry of reconciliation.

But that is what it's like to "see through a glass, darkly" (1 Cor. 13:12 KJV). We can't yet see the wonder of it all because our perspective is so limited. But Jesus sees it all. Even as he left Nazareth that day, he saw it, and he wasn't deterred or discouraged. It was the glory, the joy, "set before him" (Heb. 12:2), and he possessed that vision every step of his earthly ministry. And it is his desire that we also "catch the vision"—his vision. We will not see it all this side of heaven, but the glimpses that God has already given us of the finished work of reconciliation are probably a whole lot more than we can comprehend!

FOR FURTHER REFLECTION

1. Why did Jesus mention Naaman in this story? What do you believe he thought the Jews' reaction would be? Would you have expected an adverse reaction?
2. Why were the Jews unhappy with the prospect that the gospel was about to be spread to the Gentiles? Why did they become enraged when Jesus mentioned Naaman? Do you think the Jews believed their own writings regarding what they taught regarding the Gentile nations?
3. How can orthodoxy become a trap? Can you think of any times in the history of the church when good teaching morphed into bad religion? Why do you think this happened?
4. Why did the devil hate it when Jesus mentioned that the gospel was for the Gentiles? What were Satan's objectives? Can you see Satan doing similar things in the world today?
5. How does God use jealousy to further his kingdom purposes in the world? Do you see this as a component of his plan for redemption and reconciliation?

CHAPTER TWELVE

THE LOOK OF RECONCILIATION

BIBLICAL RECONCILIATION DEFINED IN REAL LIFE

As in so many other areas of our walk as children of God, we can get our theology straight and still miss the point. Certainly it is essential that we have biblical theology, but that is not the end of it. Good theology always leads to action. Indeed, good theology *is* action.

The ministry of reconciliation that Paul talks about is not something that can be contained in a laboratory test tube. In 2 Corinthians 5, Paul calls it the *ministry* of reconciliation, not the *theory* of reconciliation. The doctrine has legs. Many of the practical and visible characteristics of engagement in the work of reconciliation can be gleaned from the story of the slave girl. These are didactic and descriptive at the same time.

Most of us do not do well with laundry lists in learning and practicing much of anything—certainly not in our walk with the Lord. Though one wouldn't know it by looking at my desk or my bank account, I actually once read a book authored by an expert on efficiency in management. As I recall, the author set forth ten principles, most of which I have forgotten, even though while reading the book I believed I'd always remember them and they would change my life forever. I have no doubt that if I had put these ten principles into regular practice, I'd have completed my second term as president of the United States two decades ago.

But lists of dos and don'ts, even when memorized, are quickly forgotten, certainly for most of us. Such formulaic approaches are doomed from the start, particularly in kingdom work. The apostle Paul said:

> Since you died with Christ to the elemental spiritual forces of this world, why, as though you still belonged to the world, do you submit to its rules: "Do not handle! Do not taste! Do not touch!"? These rules, which have to do with things that are all destined to perish with use, are based on merely human commands and teachings. Such regulations indeed have an appearance of wisdom, with their self-imposed worship, their false humility and their harsh treatment of the body, but they lack any value in restraining sensual indulgence. (Col. 2:20–23)

Paul is talking about formulas and lists of dos and don'ts for sanctification: don't put yourself back under the law. However, he does urge us to *cultivate* godly conduct, attitudes, and habits. This transformational process, or growth, is to be accomplished only through the ongoing work of the Holy Spirit. Paul did resort to lists now and again, but the "items" on the list he calls "fruit," and it is best to understand them that way, rather than as rigid rules of conduct. Fallen man cannot bear up under such lists. Throughout human history, we have proved that we can't. We will not be transformed into the image of Christ because of New Year's resolutions. Rather, Paul says that it can be done only as we "keep in step with the Spirit":

> But the fruit of the Spirit is love, joy, peace, forbearance, kindness, goodness, faithfulness, gentleness

and self-control. Against such things there is no law. Those who belong to Christ Jesus have crucified the flesh with its passions and desires. Since we live by the Spirit, *let us keep in step with the Spirit*. (Gal. 5:22–25)

So it is in the ministry of reconciliation, in particular. We will get nowhere fast operating from a formulaic set of rules. Such an approach will always prove hollow, discouraging, and unattainable. And it has no heart.

My philosophy teacher in college taught that there are (at least) two ways to define something. One is to look at what Noah Webster has to say about it—defining things "in other words." The second is by defining something "ostensively," that is, by pointing to whatever it is that needs definition, and saying, "*That's* what it means."

He said that this is how, from infancy on, we learn to define almost everything. For example, we first learned the word *spoon* when someone pointed to the silver thing that had a long stem with a round, concave shape on the end (the dictionary definition) and said, "This is a spoon" (the ostensive definition).

Take the word *cow*. We can dictionary-define the word "until the cows come home" as a four-legged beast that has cloven hoofs, produces milk, moos, eats grass, has four stomachs, chews the cud, weighs about fifteen hundred pounds full-grown, and so on. Or we can point to a cow and say, "That's a cow." This sort of definition is much more helpful because we can literally see what it means to be a cow, and we are able to understand it in an instant.

The most meaningful way to convey what it means to participate in the ministry of reconciliation is in this way—by pointing to what it looks like as people are living it out, not by looking for a dictionary definition. We can best see what it is, and what it should be, by looking at examples. It will be a picture of what it means to "keep in step with the Spirit." There is probably no better example of this "picture definition" than Naaman's little slave girl. We can learn volumes about the ministry of reconciliation by looking at her and considering what she said and did. As lawyers are fond of saying, she would be "Exhibit A."

HUMILITY

The most striking characteristic of this young girl is her *humility*, not evident so much from what she said as from her example. It is essential that humility be taught, of course, because the Word of God does so. The Bible has a whole lot of very specific things to say about humility (many of which are taught by example). But the best way to *foster* humility is by example. The minute you try to teach or preach on the subject, it becomes difficult by its very nature, because the teacher or preacher cannot handle the subject convincingly if he or she claims expertise on what it means to be humble.

It is also a risky venture for pulpit or classroom, because the person lecturing can come off like the man who authored the book *Humility and How I Attained It*. Humility, when taught, is hard to get a handle on. It's as Lou Costello quipped in Abbott & Costello's "The Feller That Pitches for the Cleveland Indians." Abbott, beginning to be a tiny bit encouraged that maybe he had made some progress in teaching his chum Costello the distinction between Bob Feller and the rest of the "fellers" on the team: "Now you grasp it!" Costello: "Yes, I grasp it, but it keeps slipping out of my hand!"

Humility is a rare commodity in this world—particularly in politics and leadership (even in the church)—because it doesn't coordinate with the "pattern of this world" (Rom. 12:2). The world says that if you want to bring about meaningful change, you must be the boss, the king, the senator, the president, someone with real, visible power over others. Almost all of us participate in this mind-set to varied extents at the time of a presidential election: we are discouraged if our candidate loses and thrilled if he or she wins, because we think that someone in such a position will be able to truly change the world with the new authority bestowed. We would do well to look back over all elections and consider how well that has worked out!

But Jesus said, "You know that the rulers of the Gentiles lord it over them, and their high officials exercise authority over them. Not so with you. Instead, whoever wants to become great among you must be your servant, and whoever wants to be first must be your slave—just as the Son of Man did not come to be served, but to serve, and to give his life as a ransom for many" (Matt. 20:25–28). The Creator came not to be elected to a four-year term in the Oval Office, but to serve.

Contrast the slave girl with Naaman before he was healed. The world would never look at her as a change agent. On the other hand, Naaman would be a great candidate because he was in a position of authority. As the great Syrian general, he had power. He had the king's ear and thus was in a perfect spot to do something cosmic.

But not her. Indeed, if one were looking for someone who was at the very bottom of the ladder in any society, it would be hard to find someone further down than she. She was a little girl, and every hour of every day she had to endure the ignominy of being a slave. Her entire worldly existence consisted of involuntary service to others. Scripture itself indicates that such a female slave girl, in the world's estimation, is barely able to hang on to the bottom rung. In the record of the final plague on Egypt, when the Lord told Moses that all the firstborn of the people of Egypt would die, he said, "Every firstborn son in Egypt will die, from the firstborn son of Pharaoh, who sits on the throne, to the firstborn son of the female slave, who is at her hand mill" (Ex. 11:5).

But in spite of her indisputably humble status—rather, *because* of that status—she was in a perfect position to bring about substantial change as far as God was concerned. And that is the only thing that mattered.

When the Lord seeks someone to do his work, why is humility such a high priority for him? We can understand some of the reasons by looking at humility's antonym, pride. Even on its best days, pride is preachy. If I speak with a spirit of pride and superiority, even speaking the truth will be of minimal effect because I will be condescending, thus worsening the relationship. It will not so much be what I say, but who I am when I say it.

And there are many ways to convey pride and condescension, as in *false* humility. False humility is worse than blatant pride, because it is dishonest (this is obvious from the get-go). Humility is not a strategy because you can't fake it. No matter what effort one makes to appear humble, it will backfire if that person is not humble. Humility is not a tuxedo that one puts on for the occasion, but it is becoming more like Jesus,

> who, being in very nature God,
>> did not consider equality with God something to
>>> be used to his own advantage;
> rather, he made himself nothing
>> by taking the very nature of a servant,
>> being made in human likeness.
> And being found in appearance as a man,
>> he humbled himself
>> by becoming obedient to death—
>>> even death on a cross! (Phil. 2:6–8)

Naaman's slave girl was like this, being brought to nothing as Jesus was, and by becoming a servant to others as Jesus was. We must come to this ourselves if we desire to be used by God in the ministry of reconciliation. But this is impossible for us to do on our own. It cannot be done apart from the work of the Holy Spirit in us. There is one surefire way, though, to become humble. But look out!—it is dangerous (and adventurous). *Pray* for humility. If we truly want to be sanctified in this way, we must pray in faith believing: "you must believe and not doubt, because the one who doubts is like a wave of the sea, blown and tossed by the wind. That person should not expect to receive anything from the Lord" (James 1:6–7).

That's why it is dangerous, because this kind of faith is that which cries out in prayer: "No matter what it takes, Lord, make me humble like Jesus. Make me come to nothing as he came to nothing. Make me a servant to others as he was." (For those who are not 100 percent sure that God answers prayer, they should try that prayer and then watch to see what happens.) If I doubt, that is, if I am not committed to take whatever the Lord brings my way in the process, then I will be tossed about by the waves of the sea. In fact, James tells us that we can rest assured that we will *not* receive anything from the Lord.

But if I pray with faith that God will be not only my disciplinarian but my *refuge* as he works in my life to bring me these things, and that I am willing to submit to whatever he takes me through, I can be assured of something quite different: I will come out on the other side with the same mind-set as Jesus.

If Jesus had to humble himself to bring about our reconciliation both with God and with each other, we cannot do it in any other way.

By his own example, Jesus shows us that an air of superiority does not work with reconciliation. Jesus did not reach us without lowering himself to become one of us. In doing so, he humbled himself beyond anything that we can remotely imagine. We know this to be true, but we still try to preach the gospel of reconciliation without going through the messy and painful business of learning his humility in our own walk.

It may well be that the Lord, in teaching us this sort of humility, will take us through hard times that will bring us down to where the slave girl was. In fact, he almost certainly will. But what an honor to be in company with her—more than that, to be in company with Jesus. It is only when we have her humility that we can get next to others—or allow them to get next to us.

And getting next to one another in this way is almost synonymous with biblical reconciliation. It frees us up for all kinds of things—like mowing someone's lawn, cleaning toilets, volunteering for nursery duty, tutoring a special-needs child, teaching others with earnestness and credibility, and the list goes on. No one will think you unapproachable when you humbly help in these ways. It will be surprisingly and wonderfully freeing. In approaching others and when you are approached, you will be exactly where God wants you to be, so that you will be truly effective in the ministry of reconciliation.

RESPECT

Although closely tied to humility, *respect* in some ways is different, too. Like humility, it cannot be feigned. But it can be practiced. My mother, who for her entire adult life (through the very moment of the stroke that took her life at age ninety-one) taught and counseled high-schoolers, used to tell them that if they would set their feet in the right direction, their hearts would soon follow. She was right. Part of the path to true respect is treating others with respect. It makes an enormous difference in the ministry of reconciliation. And when we do not treat one another with respect, we foil the effort to reconcile at the outset.

Every human being is worthy of our respect. As Christians, we know that is true because every human being is made in the image of God. Once we get that straight in our minds, we can practice respect in our dealings with others even if we don't "feel" total respect at a given time. Genuine respect may not be there fully, but if our feet are set in the right direction, our hearts will soon follow.

When I was a seminary student, about thirty years old, I was asked to teach a Sunday school class on the book of Romans. There were approximately twenty-five adults in the class. One Sunday afternoon after class, I began to think about each member of the group, and found to my own surprise and dismay that in my mind I was "dissing" every one of them. Then I asked myself why, because I knew that such an attitude was way out of step with the Lord.

This is where respect is tied to humility, because respect simply will not exist where there is not a humble heart. Of course, the root of the problem was pride. As I reviewed my critical evaluation of each person in the class, I could see that what I was really doing was comparing that person to myself—and I wasn't being particularly objective in the process. I shouldn't have been running comparisons anyway, but in doing so I was trying to convince myself that I came out on top in every case. If I allowed respect to enter the equation, I would jeopardize my chance of coming out on top.

But Naaman's little slave girl was not haughty, and she did not diss her master. She respected him. The dictionary defines the word *respect* like this: "esteem for or a sense of the worth or excellence of a person." When she looked at her master from day to day she did so with respect and honor. This is evident from the way she approached the matter, because she spoke not directly to Naaman but to her immediate household supervisor, Naaman's wife. She respected and honored Naaman the oppressor, the slave-owner, the sinner, because the Holy Spirit had put it in her heart that Naaman was made in the image of God, just as she was.

She owed him no respect whatsoever insofar as he was a kidnapper and slave-owner, but she *did* owe him respect because he was a human being, just like her, made in the image of God. She must have been visited by an angel who handed her a prepublication draft of the book of Ephesians: "Slaves, obey your earthly masters with respect and fear, and with sincerity of heart, just as you would obey Christ" (Eph. 6:5). What? Sincerely obey and respect her owner just as she would obey *Christ*?

The gospel of reconciliation is radical. And it is impossible, until you read a bit further in Ephesians 6, where the apostle tells us that this is possible for us only if we do it as if we "were serving the Lord, not people, because you know that the Lord will reward each one for whatever good they do, whether they are slave or free" (vv. 7–8). It is a matter of faith, isn't it? Faith that God will keep his word, that we will receive our reward from him alone, and that we don't have to depend on any human agency for that to happen.

We find it relatively easy to respect those who are "respectable." Of course these would have to be "normal" human beings—such as those who are educated, work hard at their jobs, have more or less obedient kids, have no record of bad behavior (at least no worse than mine), belong to my political party, attend my church, and think just like I do. In other words, people like me. I have thus reduced respect to nothing more than worldly compatibility. This kind of respect is hollow because it is grounded in earthly values. Because it is hollow, we should not be surprised that it will evaporate in a blink when something goes awry in the relationship. It is a soap bubble, ready to pop if even a blade of grass touches it. It has nothing to sustain itself.

It is much harder to hold a "down and outer" in high esteem. He probably doesn't even hold himself in high esteem. If I am politically liberal, it may be hard for me to think highly of a conservative. If I am white, it may be hard for me to look at an African American other than paternalistically, which is the diametric opposite of respect. If I am black, I might have difficulty respecting my white coworker who I assume must be prejudiced because he is white—not even giving him a minute of time to show what his real attitudes and feelings may be.

What's worse, we tend to get comfortable with these patterns of thought and behavior because in our minds we are building and reinforcing a hierarchy of good folks and bad folks—those worthy of our respect and those unworthy. We feel more comfortable when we pigeonhole one another at the start of a relationship because it gives us something, however flimsy, to define the relationship and delivers us from the hard but happy work of developing and nurturing a Christ-centered, fulfilling relationship.

The little slave girl had developed no such hierarchy. Humanly speaking, Naaman was not worthy of her respect. But she was not "humanly" speaking when she urged her master to go down to Samaria and be healed. Like the apostle Paul, she was able to respect Naaman because she regarded "no one from a worldly point of view" (2 Cor. 5:16).

SOLIDARITY

Believers and unbelievers alike have *solidarity*, or "togetherness," in virtually every part of life. All of us need food, shelter, and clothing. We all want to be healthy. We all get the same immunizations, the same flu shots. Sinners and saints, packed together in an elevator, all hope the cable won't break, and all entertain a shared fear that it might. We all live, and we all die. Mortality tables are exactly the same for believers and unbelievers, and the death rate is still 100 percent for everybody. Jesus and the woman from Samaria both needed water to drink, and they both drank from Jacob's well.

As human beings, we are all born into the same predicament, for Jews and Gentiles alike are all under the power of sin (Rom. 3:9). But these kinds of solidarity are all passive—we have no choice in the matter. They reflect the fact that we are all human beings, thrown into the same earthly basket. Though we show universal common interests, passive solidarity is not equivalent to biblical reconciliation. The reconciliation we seek as Christians is not brought to pass by being passive in any respect, but by being intentional and proactive.

As mentioned in chapter 3, this girl was in intentional, not passive, solidarity with Naaman. She was *with* and *for* him. She shared his concern regarding his leprosy. Both of them wanted him to be healed. She did not have to do so, but she voluntarily entered his suffering. When she urged him to see the prophet in Samaria, she was absolutely united with him in the most crucial aspect of his life. Because she united with him in this interest, making it a common interest, Naaman was reconciled with Elisha and ultimately with the God of Israel.

Looking forward to Jesus, we can also see that this slave girl's initial solidarity demonstrated to Naaman was what Jesus demonstrated to Jew and Gentile alike in his earthly ministry. He shared himself in their need. He knew how people felt, what they were up against in their lives, and he was intentional in coming alongside. It was Christ's *active* obedience. He took up their burdens as his own; he cared for them; he healed them; he comforted them. He became one of us; he was *with* and *for* us:

Surely he took up our pain
 and bore our suffering,
yet we considered him punished by God,
 stricken by him, and afflicted.

But he was pierced for our transgressions,
 he was crushed for our iniquities;
the punishment that brought us peace was on him,
 and by his wounds we are healed. (Isa. 53:4–6)

This kind of solidarity is a firm foundation, being precedent to, and evidence of, true biblical reconciliation. As children of the kingdom of God seeking reconciliation, we will discover that we are gaining "unity or agreement of feeling or action; mutual support of one another" with regard to those who are already brothers and sisters in Christ *as well as with regard to those who are still unbelievers*. We know the latter is true, because Naaman was not a believer when his slave girl took up his cause. He had been "excluded from citizenship in Israel" (Eph. 2:12), but this Jewish girl did not exclude him from her world—the world of Israel, a prophet in Samaria, healing, and the God of all the earth. She urged him to go on into that world, and she walked with him as he went.

LIVING AS PEERS

Naaman's slave girl walked with him as a *peer*—not in her earthly status as a captive, but in her humanity as a member of the human race. In this sense (and this is the most important sense), they were equals. The Declaration of Independence states that it is "self-evident" that "all men are created equal" and that all "are endowed by their Creator with certain unalienable rights." I am not so sure that these maxims are as self-evident as we might like, nor that the Declaration means to say that all men will *remain* equal. Still, though imperfect, the Declaration is one of the best documents ever penned by man, and in this statement reflects the principles of Scripture.

Scripture states that "there is neither Jew nor Greek, there is neither slave nor free, there is no male and female, for you are all one in Christ Jesus" (Gal. 3:28 ESV); "they have all turned aside; together they have become corrupt; there is none who does good, not even one" (Ps. 14:3 ESV); "when a stranger sojourns with you in your land, you shall not do him wrong. You shall treat the stranger who sojourns with you as the native among you, and you shall love him as yourself, for you were strangers in the land of Egypt: I am the LORD your God" (Lev. 19:33–34 ESV). All men, women, and children are peers before the Lord.

The Bible makes it clear that this little girl and her owner were equals. There is one whole book in the Bible centered on this truth. In the book of Philemon, Paul wrote to a slave-owner after the slave, Onesimus, had bolted from his master. Onesimus then came under Paul's ministry and became a believer. Paul then beseeched his friend Philemon to take Onesimus back:

> Perhaps the reason he was separated from you for a little while was that you might have him back forever—no longer as a slave, but better than a slave, as a dear brother. He is very dear to me but even dearer to you, both as a fellow man and as a brother in the Lord. (Philem. 15–16)

Though formerly your slave, he is now your brother. He is your fellow man! Radical, amazing grace. Naaman and his slave girl were brother and sister in the Lord.

In the work of reconciliation between people of different races, this is especially important. We may eat together, attend baseball games together, and even worship together, yet not see or treat our relationships as peer relationships. A white person may think he is doing a black person a favor by companying with him, and vice versa. As mentioned before, we can become paternalistic, assuming that those of different race or country are looking to us for the answers. After all, we may think we have the answers to life's besieging issues because we live in a nicer part of town, or have a better reputation. So we assume that the members of that different race would think highly of us and look to us for leadership in helping them to get out of their circumstances.

But we are peers. There is no pecking order in the kingdom. This is a complex matter because helping others, no matter who they are, comes from a good and commendable motive. And of course it is true that when others need help, those who are in a position to give it must do so. But whether help is given or received, it is essential to recognize the other in this transaction as a peer. (When those who seem superior face needs and call for help themselves, this truth becomes wonderfully evident.)

Jesus is Lord, and yet even he considers himself our peer and treats us accordingly. Not long before he was crucified, he told his disciples that "I no longer call you servants, because a servant does not know his master's business. Instead, I have called you friends, for everything that I learned from my Father I have made known to you" (John 15:16). This is hard to comprehend, but Jesus was not exaggerating. If it was necessary for him to become our peer so that we could be reconciled to God, how can we doubt that it is necessary for us to become peers of one another as we seek reconciliation with them? We stand together at the foot of the cross, and the ground on which we stand is perfectly level.

INTRUSIVENESS

It is counterintuitive, but we must have the insight and courage to be *intrusive*. The dictionary defines *intrusive* as "disturbing another by one's uninvited or unwelcome presence." The little slave girl did not have permission to enter into Naaman's health-care world; nobody was seeking her advice. Esther did not have permission to enter the throne room of King Xerxes. Moses did not have permission to come before Pharaoh. Nathan did not have King David's permission to rebuke him. In each case, it took courage, but each intruded, uninvited, into another's world. In each case, there was significant personal risk, but it was worth the risk because of the importance of the matter at hand.

Biblical reconciliation sometimes demands this kind of intrusiveness—not an obnoxious "butting in," but courageously entering uninvited into the affairs of others. The apostle Paul commands us to "do nothing out of selfish ambition or vain conceit. Rather, in humility value others above yourselves, not looking to your own interests but *each of you to the interests of the others*" (Phil. 2:3–4). For example, when we think that someone needs help, we must not wait to be asked, and in this sense, we intrude. The need is not their business alone. It is our business, too. We do not let others just twist in the wind.

This is risky business because we can never predict what the reaction will be. Esther's, Nathan's, and the slave girl's intrusions turned out to be well received. Moses was turned away. But in each case the intruder was selfless, because if he or she had been looking only to his or her "own interests," it would have been easier and much safer to keep quiet. Esther had to consciously set aside her personal interests when she intruded on King Xerxes: "I will go to the king, even though it is against the law. And if I perish, I perish" (Esth. 4:16).

We live in a society today that despises such intrusiveness. Christians typically dislike it, too. I do. For example, when I speak with an unbeliever and have opportunity to present the gospel to him or her, why don't I realize that Paul's command "Be reconciled to God!" is the elephant in the room, and it is *essential* that I bring it up?

When I fail, it is because I don't want to intrude and I fear the response. I don't want that kind of risk in my life. Of course, I don't face anything at all like the situation that Esther faced, because I am not risking my life. But I don't want even the slightest frown to come my way. So I steer clear of the gospel and continue the discussion we were having about the weekend football game, or whether we'll get some rain tomorrow. It is much easier, and it doesn't carry the slightest bit of risk. Lord, have mercy.

As Naaman's slave girl did, we must also be willing to enter in, uninvited, when we see others in need. We should not wait to be asked. If I know someone in my congregation who cannot pay his or her rent, or has just been fired, I should collar that person and offer whatever help I can muster. In our society, that person will often be too embarrassed to ask, and his or her suffering will continue to grow if I do nothing. Indeed, my joy will be progressively diminished as well.

So it is in the reconciliation of one person to another, of one race to another, of Jew to Gentile, of rich to poor, of wife to husband, of parent to child. It often demands this kind of intrusion. Look at how Paul intruded on Philemon's business. He did so because it *wasn't* just Philemon's business, but the business of the whole family of God. Neither Philemon nor Onesimus was to be left alone. And if Naaman's slave girl had not made her master's business her business, he would not have been reconciled either to Elisha or to God.

Sometimes a different kind of intrusion is necessary. In 1955, Rosa Parks intruded on the Montgomery city bus line; Martin Luther King Jr. boycotted the same; Jackie Robinson intruded on the world of baseball in 1947. I remember those days well. At the time, most of us who lived north of the Mason-Dixon line could not see these uncomfortable intrusions as contributing to the work of racial reconciliation, but the actions ultimately did have and continue to have that effect.

All these intruders put themselves at serious personal risk, and in doing so achieved the greater good, something far beyond themselves. It is an indictment of today's church that accomplishments like this are more evident in America's city bus lines, schools, and baseball than in the church. Of course, the reconciliation we seek in Christ is everlasting and perfectly just, and it is possible only among those who believe, but we should be leading the way rather than tagging along some distance behind.

BIBLICAL RECONCILIATION
IS A HOLY WORK

Reconciliation in the kingdom of God is *holy* work. That is, we do not look to the world for its accomplishment.

In the last half-century, Christians have often done so, particularly in race relations. This is not to say that our efforts in the ministry of reconciliation will always be at loggerheads with the secular world, or that those secular efforts are wrong, but the heart of biblical reconciliation is the Word of God as applied by the Holy Spirit in our lives.

Naaman's slave girl exhibited in primitive form what this holiness looks like. Her statement, "Would that my master would see the prophet who is in Samaria! He would heal him of his leprosy" was an unmixed, uncontaminated statement of faith in the power of a supernatural God. It was a statement that by definition could not have originated from a secular or worldly source. In other words, what she claimed was sanctified. Her testimony was truly "out of this world." It was holy because it was not the wisdom of this world, but the wisdom of God:

> What we have received is not the spirit of the world, but the Spirit who is from God, so that we may understand what God has freely given us. This is what we speak, not in words taught us by human wisdom but in words taught by the Spirit, explaining spiritual realities with Spirit-taught words. The person without the Spirit does not accept the things that come from the Spirit of God but considers them foolishness, and cannot understand them because they are discerned only through the Spirit. (1 Cor. 2:12–14)

None of this is to claim that Christians have all the answers. Most secular efforts at racial reconciliation, for example, are motivated by well-meaning people who share many of our objectives. The issue is not so much the goal, but the means and the power. Take "color-blindness," a great concept and goal for anyone seeking an end to racial discrimination. We all want to get there. But it will not be realized through legislation, marches, riots, or education without the work of the Holy Spirit. We seek *biblical* color-blindness, the kind that the apostle Paul had. So we have the same goal, but radically different means. Or take the "politically correct" model, which properly posits that racial discrimination has been institutionalized. Without doubt it has been, but how to undo it, how to set it straight? Simply by empowering racial minorities? Simply by affirmative action? Simply by ending overt discrimination in the workplace and in the schools? By changing labor union rules and procedures? We should lead the way in addressing institutionalized discrimination, and can laud the efforts being made and participate in them, but anything done without the work of the Holy Spirit will prove to be a bandage, not the permanent reconciliation promised only through the blood of Christ:

> You are worthy to take the scroll
>   and to open its seals,
> because you were slain,
>   and with your blood you purchased for God
>   persons from every tribe and language and people
>   and nation.
> You have made them to be a kingdom and priests
>   to serve our God,
>   and they will reign on the earth. (Rev. 5:9–10)

So we also see something here that is utter heresy to the secular world, something that garners unmitigated hostility. Biblical reconciliation is holy. Thus, it is not inclusive. Unfortunately, this is heresy to much of the church as well, but it needs to be said. And it also needs to be understood. In one sense, there is nothing in the cosmos as all-inclusive as the kingdom of God, because no other entity or institution has its doors so wide open to every man, woman, and child—*everyone*. For *"everyone* who calls on the name of the Lord will be saved" (Joel 2:32)—no qualifications, exceptions, or exclusions.

163

All men are welcomed, urged, beseeched, and even commanded to come in ("now he commands all people everywhere to repent" [Acts 17:30]). Is there any other institution like that on earth? Yet:

> Nothing impure will ever enter it, nor will anyone who does what is shameful or deceitful, but only those whose names are written in the Lamb's book of life. (Rev. 21:27)

The holiness that the Lord requires of us in reconciliation is demonstrated most poignantly when we participate in the Lord's Supper. In it there is a warning to unbelievers as well as to unrepentant believers: they should stay away. In the same breath there is a welcome, a beseeching, to come to Christ, to repent of sin, and, in short, to be made holy. If you have brought an unbelieving friend to church that day, you likely will feel uncomfortable when the warning is given. And when we do the work of reconciliation in the church, God's holiness will often make us uncomfortable, too.

The vast majority of churches in the world today have solved this discomfort long ago by opening the Lord's Table indiscriminately. And it's tempting to do so, because we want results, we want them now, and we are going to have them, come hell or high water. But in doing so, we minimize the severe warning addressed to us in Hebrews 10:29: "How much more severely do you think someone deserves to be punished who has trampled the Son of God underfoot, who has treated as an unholy thing the blood of the covenant that sanctified them, and who has insulted the Spirit of grace?"

We may want to see success on our terms, quickly and visibly, and thus budge the door of the kingdom open beyond the Lord's prescription. But the line drawn at the Lord's Table is precisely the line drawn in biblical reconciliation. It's not our call.

Why do those of us involved in Christ-centered reconciliation so easily forget this? Why do we constantly do little more than copy worldly models and ideas? Why do we define success in worldly terms, and in accordance with secular dictates? Are we afraid that we will look foolish? Are we ashamed, and worried that the secular world will not buy into the supernatural work of the Holy Spirit in bringing to pass true reconciliation? Of *course* the world will not buy into that.

This is exactly what the apostle Paul called the "foolishness" of preaching (1 Cor. 1:21), and upon even a moment's reflection it is also exactly what we as believers truly want to buy into. The ministry of reconciliation, which Paul proclaimed as his ministry, is preaching; and like Paul, we rejoice in it even though it is utter nonsense to the secular world. Let's not worry about embarrassment before the world but be concerned about embarrassment before our God. Otherwise, our work is useless and we should forget about and abandon the whole thing. As Paul said:

> If I fought wild beasts in Ephesus with no more than human hopes, what have I gained? If the dead are not raised, "Let us eat and drink, for tomorrow we die." (1 Cor. 15:32)

We must think and speak as a child in this regard. Children have minimal fear of what people think when they speak. Of course, children often do not know what they are talking about, but we learn from them insofar as they are unabashed. They may come off as foolish, but that doesn't concern them. So it was with Naaman's little slave girl. She promised a miracle—utter foolishness to the world then, and utter foolishness to the world today. But none of the gracious, supernatural healing and reconciliation would have happened unless she had so spoken.

Holiness can be understood as looking to God alone, treating God as God. We are set apart from the world. We are altogether his and do not answer to anyone else: we have only one Person to please. To be holy means to be unmixed and uncontaminated with worldly wisdom. To the extent that we adopt secular wisdom in the ministry of reconciliation and allow it to direct our actions, and to the extent that we admit those to the fellowship of believers who do not repent, not only are we doomed to failure, but we will miss out on being a part of the wonderful, miraculous results that the Lord has promised to bring about.

A CORPORATE ENTERPRISE

As our pastors at New City Fellowship in St. Louis constantly remind us, reconciliation is a *corporate* work. We are not in it alone. The story of Naaman's slave girl exemplifies this. At first glance, what she did may not seem corporate, because we are talking about one little slave girl and one slave-owner. But a close look at the story reveals and teaches much about the nature of the body of Christ as an organism, and how its work is carried out corporately.

She is introduced to us as a young Jewish girl who had been removed from her homeland during a Syrian raid. From what she told Naaman's wife, it is clear that even at her young age she had been taught about the power of Jehovah God, and that she believed what she had been taught wholeheartedly. Though she was now in Syria where the true God was unknown, she had not forgotten her family and people, their God, or his prophet Elisha. She was still a young Jewish believer. Her body was in Damascus, but her heart was in Israel.

Her heart and her hope were inextricably tied to her family and the body of believers in her homeland. She sensed that she was not alone, and she would not have testified as she did apart from her upbringing in Israel. God's sovereignty in the matter is clearly evident, because he had arranged beforehand that this little girl would be nurtured in a believing home, that she would hear about the great prophet from others, and that she would be brought to faith herself—all of which involved the body of believers faithfully working together.

Therefore, when she spoke to Naaman's wife, she spoke out of the context of true Israel, the church, the body of Christ. She spoke *from* the church. Apart from the church where she learned about the power and mercy and healing power of Jehovah God, she could not have said what she said. She was not acting on her own, or for herself.

Further, she spoke *for* the church. In Isaiah 52:7, the prophet says, "How beautiful on the mountains are the feet of those who *bring* good news, who proclaim peace, who *bring* good tidings, who proclaim salvation." The little girl did not manufacture but *brought* good news, news that she had learned, absorbed, and believed in Israel. The gospel truth that she brought to Naaman did not originate with her. Thus her feet were on solid ground and gave her the incredible confidence to guarantee Naaman that Elisha would heal him.

We understand and rely on this truth every day in the commissioning and supporting of our missionaries sent to other lands (as she was). These missionaries are part of and speak for the body of Christ, and that sums up their work. Like her, they do not speak on their own. Their ministry is corporate.

This corporate aspect of ministry both frees the messenger, because she is not asked to rely on herself, and lends great credibility to her testimony, because the corporate witness of the world of believers underlies and gives strength to what the messenger says. Earlier in this book, we asked how it could be that Naaman's wife, Naaman himself, and King Ben-Hadad—pagans and unbelievers—so readily believed the little girl. One of the reasons was that the Holy Spirit gave them an understanding that she was speaking not on her own, but from another, very reliable source. They could tell that she was not dreaming this up. The corporate nature of her testimony came through loud and clear.

She also directed Naaman *to* the church. She did not tell him what steps he needed to take to be healed—to dip himself seven times in the Jordan. She didn't even know that. She simply sent him to Israel, to the great prophet, because she had confidence that if Naaman would just go to others in the church, he would get the help he so desperately needed. And in this case she unabashedly sent him to the very people he considered his enemies, those against whom he had waged war. Consider the result: Naaman testified, "Now I know that there is no God in all the earth except in Israel" (2 Kings 5:15). He had been admitted into membership at Elisha's church and had himself become a member of the whole body of believers, a corporate relationship.

So the little girl's work began and ended in Israel. She obtained the message there. Naaman obtained faith there. She could not have done it on her own, and Elisha could not have done it on his own either. Both of them spoke and acted from the corporate body of believers.

Particularly in America, claimed by many to have been built solely on the individual courage and vision of sturdy frontiersmen, we have succumbed to a mind-set minimizing the corporate and elevating the individual. As Frank Sinatra sang, "I did it *my* way." We love biographies of men and women who rose to the top without anyone's help, and this becomes a trap when we emulate it. Individual effort and resultant success is a virtue, no doubt, and individual responsibility was and is critical to the building of our country. But individuals do not stand alone, particularly in the church.

Do you want worry? Do you want ulcers? Do you want to feel helpless in the ministry of biblical reconciliation, in which the work seems impossible because it is so massive and impenetrable? The best way to accomplish these ends is to try to do it on your own. When we reach that point, we will come to the end of ourselves and be graciously forced to look to the Lord and his people for help. There we will find that he himself is already at work throughout the world, and that he has employed thousands of others to help. Then our individual efforts will come to life as well, because we will relax in the knowledge that God uses every effort, no matter how small or great, no matter how visible or invisible, to accomplish the already-certain work of reconciliation.

SOLID HOPE

The ministry of reconciliation is to be pursued with and characterized by *hope*—a hope not generated by our diligent work, but by the promises of God. It is the kind of hope mentioned in Hebrews 11:1—not merely a positive attitude regarding future possibilities, but a certainty. We know the endgame already. It's going to happen. It is a great expectation for all who believe.

FOR FURTHER REFLECTION

1. Discuss generally the evidences of the ministry and work of reconciliation. Have you seen such evidences in your church family?
2. Discuss the following topics as each relates to the ministry of reconciliation:
   (a) humility
   (b) respect
   (c) solidarity
   (d) living as peers
   (e) intrusiveness
   (f) holiness
   (g) corporate interdependence
3. If you can, identify and discuss examples you have seen that exhibited these characteristics, and examples that they were obviously lacking. When they were exhibited, how did they aid the ministry of reconciliation?

CHAPTER THIRTEEN

GLORIOUS EXPECTATIONS

BIBLICAL RECONCILIATION IS CERTAIN

We are not running down some rabbit trail when we work for biblical reconciliation. Because God's sovereign plans will never come up short, it is certain that ultimate, true reconciliation will absolutely be accomplished in the end. Not just reconciliation between black and white, husband and wife, warring members of the church, or liberals and conservatives. Mending these relationships is important, and we seek biblical reconciliation in every relationship, but that is not the ultimate picture.

Before we take a look at that picture (as we see it now, "through a glass darkly," like it is described in 1 Corinthians 13:12), we might again consider the exclamation of the slave girl: "If only my master would see the prophet who is in Samaria! He *would* cure him of his leprosy" (2 Kings 5:3). *Would.* Not *might*, *maybe*, or *I hope so.* The little slave girl did not carry the sophisticated baggage of doubt. Her recommendation was not nuanced. It was unqualified, straightforward, and confident—not, as Mark Twain once quipped, "mincing along with a monkey-with-a-parasol gait." She spoke boldly and did not give herself a way out. She spoke directly and guaranteed the outcome—not a guarantee from her, but a divine one.

That was faith, grounded in the power of God alone. It was the same kind of faith possessed by Abraham, who "did not waver through unbelief regarding the promise of God, but was strengthened in his faith and gave glory to God, being fully persuaded that God had power to do what he had promised" (Rom. 4:20–21).

Abraham's faith and the faith of this little girl are what we can have as we engage in the ministry of reconciliation. This faith emanates from the promises of God. This certainty is great encouragement to Christians who are making efforts to bring about biblical reconciliation. They can be absolutely assured that their efforts are not in vain, even when such efforts seem inconsequential, vague, or weak. Such efforts are certain and everlasting.

Scripture is full of descriptions of God's ultimate plan for reconciliation, and the inevitability of its accomplishment. His great plan of reconciliation is set out in Paul's letter to the church at Colossae:

For God was pleased to have all his fullness dwell in him, and through him to reconcile to himself all things, whether things on earth or things in heaven, by making peace through his blood, shed on the cross. (Col. 1:19–20)

Paul does not present this as merely possible, but certain. We can bank on it. We can work with confidence. God is doing it. He never sets out to do something that will fail. He will bring about perfect reconciliation, which has already been accomplished through the work of Christ. Paul put it in the past tense when he wrote, "All this is from God, who reconciled us to himself through Christ and gave us the ministry of reconciliation" (2 Cor. 5:18).

Since the ministry of reconciliation is from God, it will not fail. And if it will not fail, then our seemingly feeble efforts as Christians to bring it about will not fail either. God will bless those efforts, no matter how tiny and ineffectual they may seem at the moment. He will bring it to pass and let us be a part of it. He will not let our words and actions fall to the ground. Is it not infinitely better for us to be participating in an effort that is guaranteed to succeed rather than one doomed to fail?

Consider what a sure thing this is. The apostle John, recording what God showed him in the book of Revelation, tells us that he looked, and saw before him

> a great multitude that no one could count, *from every nation, tribe, people and language*, standing before the throne and before the Lamb. They were wearing white robes and were holding palm branches in their hands. And they cried out in a loud voice:
>
> "Salvation belongs to our God,
> who sits on the throne,
> and to the Lamb." (Rev. 7:9–10)

What a vision! It will be glorious. Yet it is not a vision reserved entirely for the future. Though a worship service like this will never be fully actualized on earth, we are given foretastes of it here.

RECONCILIATION ACCOMPLISHED
HERE AND NOW

Whenever the people of God assemble for worship, each worshiper is different. Whether the congregation is composed of one culture or several, there is joy in uniting in one voice, in singing together, in confessing our sins together, in testifying to the grace of God in our lives together, and in every other act of worship. It is a oneness in diversity that can be experienced only by those made one in Christ. We do not retreat from the word *diversity* because that is exactly what the Lord revealed to the apostle John in this heavenly vision.

Here on earth there is a special dimension of this kind of joy in worship. Some years ago my daughter and I went on a short-term missions trip to Ukraine. We arrived at the Donetsk airport late on a Saturday night. Having flown from St. Louis on four separate flights, we were glad to see our beds. But that respite was short, because early Sunday morning our hosts awakened us and took us to their Ukrainian Baptist Church (even though we were Presbyterian!).

At once we were surrounded by Russian-speaking Ukrainian Christians, and with the help of whispering interpreters, we were privileged to worship with them. I had never experienced anything quite like it, nor anything more joyful. Looking about at these folks while joining with them in their lusty singing of their old Russian hymns (as well as some American contemporary gospel) brought tears to my eyes, as I recognized that only a few years earlier they had lived behind the Iron Curtain and been considered our enemies.

But there was immediate commonality and joy in Christ—it was unmistakable and thrilling. It was evident that God, at that very moment, was doing what he said he would do in Paul's letter to the church at Ephesus: "For he himself is our peace, who has made the two groups one and has destroyed the barrier, the dividing wall of hostility" (Eph. 2:14). We actually got to experience that verse.

Though for many years my wife and I worshiped in churches that were white, generally of one culture, for the last decade we have worshiped at New City Fellowship in St. Louis, an intentionally cross-cultural ministry. It was a little strange for us at first because we were not accustomed to the music, clapping, hands raised in worship, and diversity of the congregation—Africans, Latinos, African Americans, Bosnians, and so forth. There were even Caucasians.

We were startled when we heard the African immigrant women embellishing the worship songs with a piercingly high-pitched trill, something that they had been accustomed to do when they met for worship in their former homeland. But it didn't take long for us to feel at home at New City, because as believers we knew that we were *already* bonded together in the family of God.

This is jaw-dropping. It is proof positive that the family of God is not tied together by culture or race, but by a unity in Christ alone. Often I glance around at the congregation during a New City worship service and am overwhelmed. Where did this come from? I feel as though I am seeing the same thing the apostle John saw on the Isle of Patmos. I have to pinch myself to remember that I haven't gone to heaven quite yet.

RECONCILIATION IS NOT A PIPE DREAM

Looking at today's world (or looking at the world at any other time in history), one might consider John's vision to be utterly fanciful—a utopia that could never exist. In Israel, Syria, Iraq, Korea, Africa—there are wars and rumors of wars. Racial division has never been worse. Every nation, tribe, people, and language? How could such reconciliation ever happen? It will happen only when we are "standing before the throne and in front of the Lamb."

When two things approach a third, they approach each other; as we approach that throne, of necessity we approach each other. Reconciliation takes place in no other manner or locale. It will happen, and it is happening. It is not something that God has reserved altogether for the future, when we will experience it fully and perfectly. The apostle Paul's command and plea is to "*be* reconciled to God" (2 Cor. 5:20). It is for us in this age, "because the kingdom of God is within you" (Luke 17:21 KJV). *Is*, not *will be.*

The great display of reconciliation that the apostle John saw before the throne of God is a grand reconciliation that has begun to take place here on earth, in real life. Children of the covenant are already filing in. Look around. Believers from every nation, tribe, people, and language are filling the sanctuary. There are Syrians, Jews, African Americans, Hispanics, Caucasians, Native Americans, Asians, Congolese, and all sorts of others.

And if you have time before the service begins, go up to the front row and introduce yourself to two folks standing together, arm in arm. It is a retired Syrian general and his one-time Jewish slave girl, waiting for Jesus to appear.

FOR FURTHER REFLECTION

1. Do you think the good news of reconciliation has both earthly and eternal significance? What Scripture supports your answer? Is reconciliation in this world important? How is it tied to God's promised eternal reconciliation?
2. How should God's promises of perfect reconciliation with him and others affect our present attitudes and behavior? How is it currently affecting yours?
3. Have you ever made an effort in spreading the gospel that seemed small and insignificant? What was it? Did it seem to you, at that time, to be important? Does the fact that God uses such acts to accomplish his great purposes in eternal reconciliation encourage you?
4. How was the slave girl's testimony used to advance God's work of reconciliation? Was it only for her and her owner, or were there ramifications beyond that relationship?
5. Do you look forward to meeting this girl in heaven? What kinds of questions will you ask her?

NOTES

CHAPTER ONE: THE STORY
1 Ricky Skaggs, "River of Jordan" (EMI Publishing, 1982).
2 William Williams, "Guide Me, O Thou Great Jehovah" (1745).

CHAPTER TWO: THE GENERAL
1 "I Sought the Lord, and Afterward I Knew" (1878).
2 John Newton, "Amazing Grace!" (1779).

CHAPTER THREE: SLAVE GIRL
1 Robert W. Johnson, ed., *The Lincoln-Douglas Debates of 1858* (New York: Oxford University Press, 2008), 319.
2 Henry F. Lyte, "Jesus, I My Cross Have Taken" (1824).
3 John Bowring, "In the Cross of Christ I Glory" (1825).
4 John Newton, "Physician of My Sin-Sick Soul" (1779).

CHAPTER FIVE: ELISHA, PART 1
1 Roland H. Bainton, *Here I Stand: A Life of Martin Luther* (Peabody, MA: Hendrickson, 2009), 49.
2 Paul Anka (words) and Claude Francois and Jacques Revaux (music), "My Way" (EMI Publishing, 1967).

CHAPTER SIX: HEALED
1 LaShun Pace, "I Know I've Been Changed" (lyrics by Peermusic Publishing, 1990).

CHAPTER SEVEN: ELISHA, PART 2
1 Westminster Shorter Catechism, Answer 4.
2 Joseph Hart, "Come, Ye Sinners, Poor and Needy" (1759).

CHAPTER EIGHT: GEHAZI AND NAAMAN
1 Joseph Hart, "Come, Ye Sinners, Poor and Needy" (1759).

CHAPTER NINE: GEHAZI AND ELISHA

1 Roland H. Bainton, *Here I Stand: A Life of Martin Luther* (Peabody, MA: Hendrickson, 2009), 49.

CHAPTER ELEVEN: JESUS AND NAAMAN

1 Joseph Hart, "Come, Ye Sinners, Poor and Needy" (1759).

INDEX OF SCRIPTURE

INDEX OF SUBJECTS
AND NAMES